ABOUT THE AUTHOR

An award-winning reporter and commentator in Detroit print and broadcast media since 1963, **George Cantor** specializes in travel and sports writing. He has written nine books on travel, including Visible Ink's *Historic Festivals* and *North American Indian Landmarks* , as well as *The Great Lakes Guidebook, Where the Old Roads Go* .

ENJOY FOOD, MUSIC & INTERESTING PLACES WITH VISIBLE INK PRESS

Food Festivals: Eating Your Way from Coast to Coast

"For anyone who finds joy in food, this is a book to savor . . . a testament to America's boundless diversity." —Jane and Michael Stern, authors of *Eat Your Way Across the U.S.A.*

This tantalizing travel guide gives mouth-watering details of over 400 of the biggest, best and most unusual food festivals in America, such as the Maine Lobster Festival to California's Gilroy Garlic Festival and the World's Biggest Fish Fry in Paris, Tennessee.

Barbara Carlson • 400 pages • 75 photos • ISBN 1-57859-003-5

Music Festivals from Bach to Blues

"A unique listener's guide to all genres of tuneful revelry across North America."—*Time International*

Music Festivals takes you coast to coast, exploring the full spectrum of North American music festivals, including the Chicago Gospel Festival, New York's Lake George Opera Festival, and the South by Southwest Music and Media Conference in Austin, Texas.

Tom Clynes • 632 pages • 140 photos • ISBN 0-7876-0823-8

Historic Festivals: A Traveler's Guide

"Takes travelers on an entertaining coast-to-coast tour celebrating the richness of America's cultural heritage." —*Time International*

Journey across the U.S. with *Historic Festivals*, celebrating the nation's history with visits to such events such as Florida's Gasparilla Pirate Invasion, Iowa's Steamboat Days, and the Boston Tea Party Reenactment in Massachusetts.

George Cantor • 392 pages • 100 photos • ISBN 0-7876-0824-6

WHERE TO

Gamble

WHERE TO

Gamble

A GUIDE TO CASINOS, RIVERBOATS, RESERVATIONS, RACETRACKS AND MORE

George Cantor

VISIBLE
INK
PRESS

Detroit   New York   Toronto   London

WHERE TO
GAMBLE : A Guide to Casinos, Riverboats,
Reservations, Racetracks and More

Copyright © 1998, Visible Ink Press™

Published by **Visible Ink Press™**
a division of Gale Research
835 Penobscot Building
Detroit, MI 48226-4094

Visible Ink Press™ is a trademark of Gale Research

Most Visible Ink Press™ books are available at special quantity discounts when purchased in bulk by corporations, organizations, or groups. Customized printings, special imprints, messages, and excerpts can be produced to meet your needs. For more information, contact the Special Markets Manager at the above address. Or call 1-800-877-4253.

Art Directors: Pamela A.E. Galbreath, page design; Mary Krzewinski, cover design
Typesetting: Marco Di Vita, Graphix Group
Cover photos: Super Stock and AP Wide World

Library of Congress Cataloging-in-Publication Data
Cantor, George, 1941–
        Where to gamble : a guide to casinos, riverboats, reservations, racetracks and more/by George Cantor
            p. cm.
        Includes index.
        ISBN 1-57859-022-1 (alk. paper)
            1. Gambling—United States. 2. Casinos—United States—Directories. 3. Riverboats —United States—Directories. 4. Racetracks (Horse racing)—United States—Directories. 5. Jai alai —United States—Directories. 6. Lotteries —United States— Directories. I. Title.
        GV1301.C275   1997
        795'.025'73—dc21   97-37393
                                                                                    CIP

TO SHERRY,
DRAWING TO A FULL HOUSE.

A DOLPHIN JUMPS OUT OF THE POOL AT THE MIRAGE IN LAS VEGAS. (COURTESY OF THE MIRAGE)

Contents

CONTENTS

GAMBLING IN AMERICA

First it was just Nevada. For the best part of five decades in America, if you wanted to put down a legal bet in a casino you had to go west.

It made some kind of demographic sense. In 1931, Nevada was a big empty hole in the map with not much going for it. Its mines were played out, water was scarce, and the country was locked in the Depression. It was a time for desperate measures.

Over the years, the state built up two of the greatest entertainment districts the country had ever seen. Being right next door to California during the era of that state's greatest growth and prosperity didn't hurt much, either. As package charters put air travel within reach of most Americans, the entire country opened up, as well.

In those years, traveling to Las Vegas or Reno was a special adventure. The visitor had the sense that this was different, unlike any other place he had ever seen. From the slot machines at the airport, to the glittering signs on the strips, to the show business legends in the big hotels, this wasn't anything like home. Self-contained and unique, the Nevada desert seemed like an oasis of gambling interests.

As a travel writer, I have never seen any aspect of the travel business change as quickly. In the '90s, casinos are suddenly everywhere. On Indian reservations. In the big cities of the Midwest. In the Bible Belt South.

With bewildering speed, casinos are opening up almost every other month, in places that seemed like the most improbable venues. It used to be that when you got to Las Vegas you knew you weren't in Kansas anymore. Now casinos are right across the river from Kansas. You can see them from the river boat.

This travel guide, *Where to Gamble*, was the most difficult I ever put together, simply because the industry is changing so rapidly. Although I sometimes had the feeling that I was trying to catch fireflies with a cookie jar, I have attempted to include the best places to gamble in the U.S., as accurately and completely as possible. When you're ready for some fresh air and sunlight, *Where to Gamble* also includes some interesting museums, parks and festivals to catch while you're visiting the area. Gambling venues have become the theme parks of the '90s, offering wide selections of family fare, in addition to the standard gaming tables.

The expansion has not come cost free. The horse racing industry has been badly hurt. As I write this, it was announced that one of the country's historic tracks, Arlington Park, near Chicago, will shut down because it cannot compete with new Illinois casinos. Cities like New Orleans, Kansas City and St. Louis, which rested downtown development hopes on casinos, have found that gambling as a tourist attraction and economic boost is not quite the sure bet is seemed. This has not deterred Detroit, the largest American city to approve casinos, to try the same strategy and its casinos are scheduled to open before the end of the century. While gambling is usually promoted as a boon to job growth, areas near casinos have seen a rise in personal bankruptcies and some evidence of increases in crime and divorce.

At the same time, a number Native American tribes have been enriched by casino gaming beyond anything they could have imagined—creating new jobs, educational opportunities for their children, a dignified life. Millions of people who enjoy gambling as a recreation have been given the opportunity to participate in what, by and large, is a harmless pursuit.

Moralists claim, however, that gambling goes counter to the work ethic and instructs people that it is, indeed, possible to get something for nothing. A backlash has developed against further expansion, and in 1997 a national commission was formed to seriously investigate the industry for the first time.

Still, Americans seem to be pulling the lever on slots more enthusiastically than they ever did on voting machines. Las Vegas is thriving as never before, as many people who get a taste of casinos on their home turf decide they now want a taste of the "real thing." The industry that began out of desperation in the desert in 1931 has now become the biggest travel commodity in the country. *Where to Gamble* is an encyclopedia of this culture, taking you to places familiar and new. It's a safe bet that it will bring more power to your dollar.

ACKNOWLEDGMENTS

Thanks to the following people for making *Where to Gamble* a sure bet:

Visible Ink art directors Pamela A. E. Galbreath and Mary Krzewinski for patience and creativity during the page and cover design process.

Marco Di Vita of the Graphix Group for typesetting yet another Visible Ink Press title faster than the speed of light.

Maria Franklin and Michelle Lonoconus for securing photo permissions.

Randy Bassett, Pam Reed, and Gary Leach in Gale's Graphic Services Department for sizing and cropping photos, printing negatives, and creating regional maps.

Carole Craddock for the lowdown on Vegas.

Complimentary photographs were received from these gaming establishments:

The Alton Belle in Alton, Illinois; The Belle of Baton Rouge in Baton Rouge, Louisiana; Diamond Jo Casino in Dubuque, Iowa; The Golden Nugget Hotel & Casino in Las Vegas, Nevada; Grand Casino Mille Lacs in Onamia, Minnesota; Harrah's Ak-Chin Casino in Maricopa, Arizona; The Luxor in Las Vegas, Nevada; The MGM Grand Hotel, Casino & Theme Park in Las Vegas, Nevada; The Mirage in Las Vegas, Nevada; Treasure Island in Las Vegas, Nevada; Turning Stone Casino in Verona, New York.

HOW TO USE THIS BOOK

In *Where to Gamble: A Guide to Casino, Riverboats, Reservations, Racetracks and More,* entries are arranged first by region, then alphabetically by state, and then alphabetically by establishment name. Icons indicate the type of gaming establishment.

 State Lotteries: State lottery information appears at the beginning of each state's chapter.

 Jai Lai: Available only in Florida, jai alai is a face-paced court game similar to handball played usually by two to four players with a ball and a long curved wicker basket strapped to the wrist.

 Casinos: Casinos offer a wide variety of gaming, including blackjack, roulette, poker, slots, bacarrat, keno, craps, video poker, video keno, caribbean stud poker and pai gow poker.

 Riverboats: Casinos on the water, riverboats offer the ambiance of a bygone era. Some riverboats never leave port.

 Indian Reservations: In 1988, the Indian Gaming Regulatory Act allowed federally registered tribes to open gaming operations after signing an agreement with the state in which they are located. There are large-scale gaming facilities run by the Native American tribes in many states, including Michigan, Minnesota, Wisconsin and the Dakotas.

 Racetracks: Listings are included for both harness racing and thoroughbred racing.

The entries in *Where to Gamble* highlight the best gaming establishments in the United States. Since there are so many casinos in Las Vegas and Atlantic City, the **appendix** offers a complete list of casinos in both cities. For a list of gambling terms, consult the **glossary.** The **indexes** list the names of establishments, prominent people in the gaming industry and other sites to see.

NORTHEAST

Connecticut
Delaware
Maine
Maryland
Massassachusetts
New Hampshire
New Jersey
New York
Pennsylvania

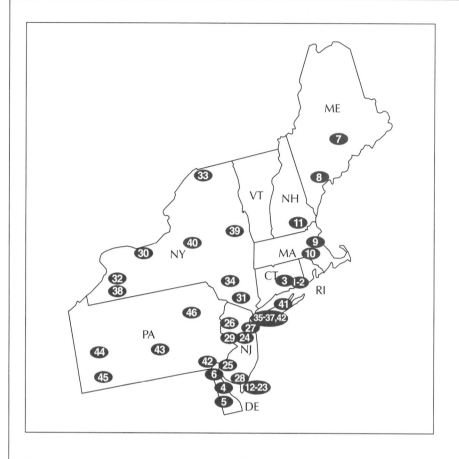

Connecticut

1. Foxwoods Casino, Ledyard
2. The Cinetropolis at Foxwoods, Ledyard
3. Mohegan Sun Casino, Norwich

Delaware

4. Dover Downs, Dover
5. Midway Slots at Harrington Raceway, Harrington
6. Delaware Park, Wilmington

Maine

7. Bangor Raceway, Bangor May
8. Scarborough Downs, Scarborough

Massachusetts

9. Suffolk Downs, Boston
10. Foxboro Park, Foxboro

New Hampshire

11. Rockingham Park, Salem

New Jersey

12. Bally's Park Place, Atlantic City
13. Caesar's Atlantic City
14. Claridge's, Atlantic City
15. The Grand-Bally, Atlantic City
16. Merv Griffin's Resort, Atlantic City
17. The Sands, Atlantic City
18. The Showboat, Atlantic City
19. TropWorld Casino & Entertainment Resort, Atlantic City
20. Trump Plaza Hotel & Casino, Atlantic City
21. Trump's Taj Mahal Casino Resort, Atlantic City
22. Harrah's Casino Hotel, Atlantic City
23. Trump's Castle Casino Resort, Atlantic City

Connecticut

In Connecticut, gaming is limited to two casinos run by the Pequot and Mohegan tribes. For state lottery information, contact the Connecticut State Lottery.

 Connecticut State Lottery, 85 Alumni Road, Newington 06111, (860)667-5180. Sales: $707 million. Proceeds: $262 million. 100% General Fund.

LEDYARD

The greatest success story of tribal gaming in the United States, Foxwoods has become the largest casino-hotel complex in the Northeast and a tourist magnet for the entire area between New York City and Boston. It is the biggest and most profitable casino in the country. There are actually two casinos, one for non-smokers, on the site, along with three hotels, sixteen restaurants and a showroom with name entertainment. Connecticut receives more revenue from the casino than any other enterprise in the state.

The Pequot historically were wiped out 1637, as part of a bitter struggle with British colonists and the Mohegan, with whom they had split around 1600. They occupied the entire Thames Valley of eastern Connecticut at the peak of their power. By the twentieth century, however, they were reduced to two small bands holding tiny tracts in the area. The Pequot have opened membership to anyone who can prove one-sixteenth ancestry. The casino has enabled the tribe to extend comprehensive educational and health care benefits to all its members.

 Foxwoods Casino, *(Mashantucket Pequot Tribe).* On Connecticut 2, nine miles east of the Westerly, Rhode Island, exit of I-95. (203)885-3000. Open daily, twenty-four hours. Offers 3,864

THE FOXWOODS RESORT IN LEDYARD, CONNECTICUT. (AP WIDE WORLD, NORWICH BULLETIN)

slots, 707 video poker machines, 106 blackjack tables, twenty-four craps tables, twenty roulette tables, six pai gow poker tables, forty-seven poker tables, seventy keno seats, ten video keno machines, sixteen caribbean stud poker tables, big six, baccarat, and red dog. There are also 1,250 seats for bingo. The hotel offers an indoor pool and a number of restaurants: Cedars Steak House, Han Garden, Al Dente, Pequot Grill, Festival Buffet, The Deli, Branches at Two Trees Inn, Pizza Plus, Expresso Deli, the Atrium Lounge, Aces Up Lounge, High Stakes Cafe, and a Sports Bar.

 # The Cinetropolis at Foxwoods

Visitors to Foxwoods should see The Cinetropolis. **The Cinedrome 360** is a movie theater in the round that surrounds visitors with state-of-the-art visuals and sounds. Viewers can enjoy "Virtual Vacations" or the time travel experience. At night, the theater turns into a dance club. Groups of six people journey beneath the sea to save the eggs of the Loch Ness Monster in just one of the **Virtual Adventures,** virtual reality rides. **Turbo Ride** takes viewers on an intense ride at the movies with hydraulic seats—takeoffs, liftoffs and G-forces are all part of the action-packed experience.

THE SLOT MACHINES AT THE MOHEGAN SUN CASINO. (AP WIDE WORLD, JOHN SHISHMANIAN)

NORWICH

Opened in late 1996, the Mohegan owners of this casino sought to emulate the success of the neighboring Pequot, their ancient enemies. The Mohegan, under the great strategist and war leader, Uncas, broke away from the Pequot at the start of the seventeenth century. Through a series of alliances with the British, they became the most powerful tribe in southern New England by the end of the century. But land-hungry settlers forced their transport to New York, and from there to Wisconsin. Only a few hundred remained in Connecticut and most were absorbed by the white population.

 Mohegan Sun Casino, *(Mohegan Tribe of Connecticut).* (860)886-9338.

Delaware

After gambling was legalized in neighboring New Jersey, Delaware race track operators complained they could not compete unless given the right to bring some form of casino action onto their properties. So the state allowed three tracks to include slots and off-track video betting. For lottery information, contact the the Delaware State Lottery.

 Delaware State Lottery, 1575 Mckee Road, Suite 102, Dover 19904, (302)739-5291. Sales: $111 million. Proceeds: $37 million. 100% General Fund.

DOVER

 Dover Downs. Just north of Dover, on U.S. 13, (302)674-4600. Simulcasts and harness races run from November–April. Monday to Saturday, 8 a.m.–2 a.m.; Sunday, open 1 p.m. Also hosts NASCAR racing events during the summer. Offers 1,000 slots.

HARRINGTON

 Midway Slots at Harrington Raceway. Eighteen miles south of Dover, on U.S. 13, on the Delaware State Fairgrounds. (888)88-SLOTS. Racing simulcasts run Monday to Saturday, 8 a.m.–2 a.m.; open Sunday at 1 p.m. 500 slot machines.

WILMINGTON

 Delaware Park. North from exit 4B of I-95, by way of Delaware 7; eleven miles southwest of downtown Wilmington,

THE SMOKE-FREE SLOT MACHINE AREA AT DOVER DOWNS. (AP WIDE WORLD, GARY EMEIGH)

(302)994-2521. Simulcasts, slots, video poker, and thoroughbred racing April–November. Monday to Saturday, 8 a.m.–2 a.m.; open Sunday at 1 p.m.

Maine

With the exception of horse racing, there are no other gaming facilities in Maine. To obtain lottery information, contact the Maine State Lottery.

 Maine State Lottery, 10-12 Water Street, Hallowell 04333, (207)287-3721. Sales: $148 million. Proceeds: $39 million. 96% General fund; 4% Outdoor Fund.

BANGOR MAY

 Bangor Raceway, harness racing. (207)942-9000. Races run late May–July.

SCARBOROUGH

 Scarborough Downs. On U.S. 1, at the Scarborough exit of the Maine Turnpike, (207)883-4331. Races run March–November.

Maryland

Gaming in Maryland is limited to harness and thoroughbred racing, and lottery tickets. For more information about the lottery, contact the Maryland State Lottery.

 Maryland State Lottery, 6776 Reisterstown Road, Suite 204, Baltimore 21215, (410)764-5700. Sales: $1.1 billion. Proceeds: $392 million. 100% General fund.

BALTIMORE

Home of the Preakness Stakes, the second jewel in racing's triple crown, held on the third Saturday of May. The first Preakness was held in 1873, two years before the Kentucky Derby. But because there was a gap of three years in the 1890s, the Derby actually has been run once more often.

 Pimlico, thoroughbred track. Park Heights and Belvedere Avenues, west from I-83 on the Northern Parkway, in the northwest part of the city. (410)542-9400. Daily mid–March to early June and late July to late September.

LAUREL

 Laurel Park, thoroughbred track. Off U.S. 1, about midway between Baltimore and Washington. From Baltimore, exit I-95 at Maryland 32, head east and then south on U.S. 1. From Washington, exit I-95 at Maryland 198, head east and then north on U.S. 1. A favorite track for capital politicians, Laurel has held meets since the Taft administration. Star attraction is The International, featuring horses from around the world. Daily, October to mid–March. (301)725-0400.

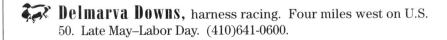

OCEAN CITY

Delmarva Downs, harness racing. Four miles west on U.S. 50. Late May–Labor Day. (410)641-0600.

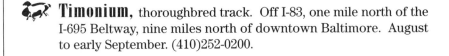

OXON HILL

Rosecroft Raceway, harness racing. South of exit 4A on the Capital Beltway (I-95, 495); eight miles southeast of downtown Washington, D.C. All year, except Monday and Christmas week. (301)567-4000.

TIMONIUM

Timonium, thoroughbred track. Off I-83, one mile north of the I-695 Beltway, nine miles north of downtown Baltimore. August to early September. (410)252-0200.

Massachusetts

In Massachusetts, gambling is limited to placing bets at the track, and purchasing lottery tickets. For information about the lottery, contact the Massachusetts State Lottery.

 Massachusetts State Lottery, 60 Columbian Street, Braintree 02184, (617)849-5555. Sales: $3 billion. Proceeds: $443 million. 100% City-town general fund budgets.

BOSTON

 Suffolk Downs, thoroughbred track. Off Massachusetts 1A, at Massachusetts 145; four miles north of Boston, just beyond Logan International Airport. (617)727-2581. January–June.

FOXBORO

 Foxboro Park, thoroughbred track. Off I-95 at the Foxboro exit; thirty-one miles southwest of downtown Boston. (508)543-3800. April–October.

New Hampshire

Gambling in New Hampshire is limited to betting at the track and lottery tickets. For state lottery information, contact the New Hampshire State Lottery.

 New Hampshire State Lottery, 75 Fort Eddy Road, Concord 03301, (603)271-3391. Sales: $166 million. Proceeds: $50 million. 100% education.

SALEM

 Rockingham Park, thoroughbred track. Off I-93 at the Salem exit; nine miles north of Lawrence, Massachusetts. (603) 898-2311. June–October.

New Jersey

In 1976, Las Vegas-style gambling in Atlantic City was approved by the New Jersey legislature. Lottery information can be obtained by contacting the New Jersey State Lottery.

 New Jersey State Lottery, Brunswick Avenue Circle, Lawrenceville 08648, (609)599-5800. Sales: $1.6 billion. Proceeds: $662 million. 63% state institutions; 37% education.

ATLANTIC CITY

For nearly a century this was America's top summer resort. Atlantic City was never a place with the cachet of a Newport or a Bar Harbor. No, this was democracy at play, with no pretensions and very few airs, except those wafting in from the sea.

It was salt water taffy and rolling chairs. It was the first picture postcards in America for the envious folks back home. It was horses diving forty-five feet into the water at the Steel Pier. It was pretty girls in swimsuits trying to become the sweetheart of the nation. Sheltered from northern storms by the curve of the New Jersey coastline, closer to the warm water of the Gulf Stream than any other resort in the North, Atlantic City basked in sun that never failed. And on days when it did, there was always the Boardwalk, an endless carnival of rare delights to buy and to gawk at. In the years before World War II, it attracted sixteen-and-a-half million visitors annually. They came to splash in the surf, marvel at the crowds, seek the love of their lives and go home sunburned and sated. "On the Boardwalk in Atlantic City, life will be peaches and cream," went a song of the times. No one believed otherwise.

It had been that way almost from the first day the railroad came through, in 1854. Investors saw the potential of Absecon Island, an empty, windswept, swampy piece of real estate. They joined it to the mainland by bridge, called it a resort and built the railroad from Camden. Acceptance was immediate. Many Southern families spent the summers there in its first years. But it was after the Civil War that Atlantic City attained its greatest growth. It was an easy weekend destination for the millions of New York City and Philadelphia. The first Boardwalk, which opened in 1870, set the tone. It was a device to gather the crowds, not to keep them out, as was the case in the more upscale resorts. While the city-bound visitors liked to say that they were "getting away" for the weekend, what really drew them was the urban excitement of the Boardwalk, set in a healthful environment cooled by the sea breezes.

By the 1920s, when the Miss America Pageant was started as a device to extend the summer season past Labor Day, the basic elements that defined Atlantic City were all in place. But within thirty years, it began to change. Affordable air travel and the Interstate highway system brought more distant places within easy reach. A sophisticated traveling public, who already had seen all that Atlantic City had to offer on their TV sets, began looking for other summer diversions. Despite repeated promises by community leaders to diversify, Atlantic City remained totally dependent upon its resort facilities. It was a formula for disaster. By the 1970s, the flood of visitors had dried to a trickle, and those who did come were not the big spenders of old. The unskilled labor that was drawn to the place because of regular work soon became a reservoir of the almost permanently unemployed. In an act of desperation the state approved casino gambling in 1978 for its stricken star resort.

The results are still open to debate. Once more, Atlantic City is the top tourist draw in New Jersey. An estimated thirty million visitors a year come here. But this total includes day trippers who arrive only to play in the casinos and then depart. The row of blocks behind the glittering hotel-casinos remains blighted. Relatively few of the town's impoverished residents were able to find employment. The economic spinoff has been negligible.

The Marina area, developed in the hopes of expanding the casinos in an area apart from The Boardwalk, has attracted just two hotels. But this is where most of the available land is situated and in the late 90s several family-themed resorts were discussing the possibility of locating there.

On the Boardwalk, the beat of life has returned. Ten of the dozen casinos licensed for the city are concentrated there and they have brought a measure of excitement back to the old planking. Aging hotels were torn down and replaced by glitzy, new, high-rise complexes, most of them featuring several restaurants, showrooms, indoor sports facilities and improved beaches. Big name entertainers again appear. Maybe it isn't the peaches and cream of the past, but having scraped the empty bowl, Atlantic City is happy with the dish it has today.

The Casinos: all operate daily, twenty-four hours. By law they must have an attached hotel of at least 500 rooms. Ten are located on the Boardwalk, and two near Brigantine Boulevard, west of downtown. These are enormous operations, with an average of fifty blackjack tables, 1,500 slot machines and a dozen craps tables. The minimum bet at most tables at most times is $5, with a maximum of $5,000. There is no sports book or bingo, but most variations of poker and simulcast horseracing is offered.

ATLANTIC CITY: BOARDWALK-AREA CASINOS

Bally's Park Place. Park Place and the Boardwalk. A forty-nine-story high rise with indoor pool, exercise room and beach. Show room with big name headliners. 2,000 slots, fifty-six blackjack tables, fourteen craps tables, twenty-four poker tables and fifty-seven keno seats. (609)340-2000, (800)772-7777.

Caesar's Atlantic City. Pacific and Arkansas Avenues. Nineteen stories, on the ocean. Exercise room, miniature golf, tennis courts, private beach, and the Appian Way Shopping Promenade. Caesars Circus Maximus Theater seats 1,006 spectators for musical productions, sporting events and special performances.. In the regular casino, there are almost 2,000 slots, forty-six blackjack tables, thirteen roulette tables, seventy keno seats. There are also slot machines available in a non-smoking casino. (609)348-4411, (800)443-0104.

Claridge's. Across Brighton Park from the Boardwalk, between Park Place and Indiana Avenue. Indoor pool, exercise room. (609)340-3400.

The Grand-Bally. Boston and Pacific Avenues, at the extreme southern end of the casino area. Beachfront, twenty-three stories. Indoor pool, entertainment. 1,800 slots, fifty-one blackjack tables, fourteen craps tables, twenty-nine keno seats. (609)347-7111.

Merv Griffin's Resort. Boardwalk at North Carolina Avenue. Nine–fifteen stories, beachfront. The first casino in Atlantic City, offers guests an indoor/outdoor pool, private beach area, exercise room, amusement arcade and big name entertainment in the 1,400-seat Superstar Theatre. Fifty blackjack tables, 2,000 slots, twelve craps tables. (609)344-6000, (800)336-MERV.

THE FORTY-TWO STORY TRUMP TAJ MAHAL OVERLOOKS THE ATLANTIC CITY BOARDWALK. (AP WIDE WORLD, DON SLABICKI)

The Sands. Adjoining Brighton Park, one block west of the Boardwalk, at Indiana Avenue and Dr. Martin Luther King, Jr. Boulevard. Twenty-one stories, on the ocean. Exercise room. 1,700 slots, fifty-one blackjack tables, twelve craps tables. (609)441-4000.

The Showboat. Boardwalk and Delaware Avenue, at the northern end of the casino area. Twenty-four stories, on the ocean. Bowling center, exercise room. (609)343-4000, (800)621-0200 for reservations.

TropWorld Casino & Entertainment Resort. Boardwalk and Brighton Avenue. Twenty-three stories on the ocean; indoor pool and amusement park, exercise room. (609)340-4000, (800)257-6227.

Trump Plaza Hotel & Casino. Boardwalk and Mississippi Avenue. Thirty-five stories, all ocean view, beachfront, entertainment. (609)441-6000, (800)677-7787, reservations.

Trump's Taj Mahal Casino Resort. Boardwalk at the Steel Pier, between Pennsylvania and Virginia Avenue. Fifty-one stories, 1,250 guest rooms, including 237 suites with the most lavish facilities and distinctive architecture on the Boardwalk, a mixture of Indian and contemporary design. Nine restaurants, three ballrooms, indoor pool, Jacuzzis, on the ocean, exercise room. Guests can enjoy sporting competitions, concerts, and other live entertainment in the 5,000-seat Mark G. Estess Arena. As one of the largest casinos in the world, the Taj Mahal offers over 3,000 slot machines, fifty-eight poker tables, and 160 table games. (609)449-1000.

ATLANTIC CITY: OFF BOARDWALK AREA

Harrah's Casino Hotel. 1725 Brigantine Boulevard. Sixteen stories, 760 rooms. Transportation to Boardwalk area. Indoor pool, Jacuzzi, sauna, golf course, shopping arcade, exercise room. Features a company-owned and -operated dockside marina. Live entertainment at the Atrium Lounge and The Broadway by the Bay Theatre. Over 2,000 slots, fourteen roulette tables, forty-eight 21 tables, in addition to other table games. (609)441-5000, (800)2-HARRAH.

Trump's Castle Casino Resort. On New Jersey 87 (Brigantine Boulevard) one mile north of U.S. 30, at the Frank S. Far-

The Miss America Pageant

All promoters wanted to do was make summer one week longer and persuade the crowds to remain in Atlantic City beyond the traditional Labor Day close of the season. What they did was create an institution.

Atlantic City has changed completely, from the country's most popular beach resort to a rather blowsy gambling town. Standards for what makes an ideal face and form have been altered a dozen times. The Miss America pageant has been reviled by feminists, parodied by comics, imitated by competitors. Yet it remains securely a piece of Americana. People who scoff at and ignore other such competitions still read about Miss America, and the stories about the pageant remain front-page news in most papers in the country.

It began in 1921 as almost an afterthought, just another in a series of promotions. The next two years, in fact, the same young woman, Mary Campbell, of Columbus, Ohio, won the title, the only repeat performance in the pageant's history and unthinkable under current rules. It was all just fun and froth, and when the contest was briefly discontinued in the late 1920s, it wasn't missed by many.

But after Atlantic City felt the bite of the Depression, it revived the competition in 1933. It was formalized, given some style, elevated to a show that considered factors beyond mere beauty. And it caught on. A few winners—Bess Myerson, Lee Meriweather, Marilyn Van Derbur, Vanessa Williams—all went on to successful show business careers. But most returned to a life of only local celebrity after their season in the spotlight. The pageant has also become a barometer of changes in the national attitude. African Americans have won and, in 1994, a deaf woman was crowned Miss America, far cries from the splashing flappers of the 1920s.

The Miss America Pageant is held the weekend after Labor Day at the Convention Center, on the Boardwalk between Mississippi and Florida Avenues. The pageant includes a parade, entertainment, and scheduled appearances by contestants. For more information, contact the Miss America Pageant Organization, P.O. Box 119, Atlantic City 08404, (609)344-5278. (From *Historic Festivals: A Traveler's Guide*, by George Cantor, Visible Ink Press, 1996)

ley Marina. Twenty-seven stories, over 700 guest rooms, overlooking Absecon Bay and the 640-slip Senator Frank S. Farley State Marina. Trump's Castle Casino has a medieval theme, and features a wide variety of amenities, including nine restaurants; Viva's Nightclub; Captain's Lounge (seasonal); the 462–seat King's Court Showroom; 21,400 square feet to enjoy in the Crystal Ballroom; and a 3.17 acre recreation deck with tennis and shuffleboard courts, miniature golf, an exercise room and basketball. The casino offers 2,100 slots, forty-three blackjack tables, fourteen craps tables, twelve roulette tables, six poker tables, and the One Race Book Parlor—a sports book with twenty-six mounted TVs, forty-two individual TVs showing races from around the nation, seven betting windows and automated betting machines. (609)441-2000, (800)365-8786.

FREEHOLD

Freehold Raceway, harness racing. At U.S. 9 and New Jersey 33; thirty-two miles south of Elizabeth. August–December. (201)462-3800.

CHERRY HILL

Garden State Park, thoroughbred track. Off New Jersey 70; six miles east of downtown Philadelphia by way of the Benjamin Franklin Bridge. January–June. (609)488-8400.

EAST RUTHERFORD

Meadowlands Race Track, thoroughbred track. At the Meadowlands Sports Complex exit of the New Jersey Turnpike (I-95). The track is part of the Meadlowlands complex, which also includes Giants Stadium and the Brendan Byrne Arena. Open all year. (201)935-8500.

LONG BRANCH

The original Monmouth Park racetrack on the site dates from 1870, when Long Branch was the most fashionable of the New Jersey beach resorts for New Yorkers. The race meets rivaled those at Saratoga in color and the Social Register attendees. Seven presidents made Long Branch their summer home from U.S. Grant to Woodrow Wilson.

Monmouth Park, thoroughbred track. West on New Jersey 35, in Oceanport. The season runs daily, early June to early September. (908)222-5100.

MCKEE CITY

 Atlantic City Race Course, thoroughbred track. At the junction of U.S. 40 and 322; fourteen miles west of Atlantic City. Daily, June–early September. (609)641-2190.

New York

Gaming in New York is available at Native American owned casinos and betting at the racetrack. For state lottery information contact the New York State Lottery.

 New York State Lottery, 1 Broadway Center, Schenectady 12301, (518)388-3300. Sales: $3.7 billion. Proceeds: $1.4 billion. 100% education.

BATAVIA

 Batavia Downs, harness racing. South from exit 48 of the New York Thruway; thirty-seven miles southwest of downtown Rochester. August–October. (716)343-3750.

FARMINGTON

 Finger Lakes, thoroughbred track. South from New York Thruway exit 44, at junction of New York 96 and 322; twenty-seven miles southeast of Rochester. April–December. (716)924-3232.

GOSHEN

The birthplace of American harness racing, this is a registered National Historic Landmark. Racing has been traced back to 1838 on this site. The adjacent Museum of the Trotter is housed in the original stables. The museum is being renovated.

 Historic Goshen Track, harness racing. North from U.S. 6 on New York 207, to Park Place; six miles east of Middletown. Call for hours at (914)294-6330. The Goshen meet runs daily, from mid-May to mid-July. (914)294-5333.

UNBRIDLED'S SONG, WITH JOCKEY MIKE SMITH ABOARD, BEGINS TO OPEN A LEAD AT THE AQUEDUCT RACE TRACK. (AP WIDE WORLD, JOHN DUNN)

HAMBURG

 Buffalo Raceway, harness racing. South from exit 56 of the New York Thruway at the Erie County Fairgrounds; thirteen miles south of downtown Buffalo. January–July, October–December. (716)649-1280.

HOGANSBURG

The Mohawk were the easternmost members of the Iroquois Confederacy and dominated the land that is now New York between the Mohawk and Saint Lawrence Rivers. Supporters of the British in colonial struggles with the French, they continued the alliance during the American Revolution. As a result, most of the tribe was forced to move to Canada after 1783. Land was set aside for them in Ontario and Quebec. This reserve is on the Canadian border and is the only tribal remnant still in the United States.

 Mohawk Bingo Palace, *(St. Regis Mohawk Tribe.)* Ten miles south of Cornwall, Ontario, Canada. (518)358-2246.

MONTICELLO

 Monticello Raceway, harness racing. West on New York 17B, off New York 17; twenty-five miles northwest of Middletown. All year. (914)794-4100.

NEW YORK CITY

 Aqueduct, thoroughbred track. In the Borough of Queens, off the Belt Parkway, just west of I-678 and Kennedy Airport. Daily, January–May and October–December. (718)641-4700.

 Belmont, thoroughbred track. In Nassau County, just east of the Hempstead Turnpike exit of the Cross Island Parkway. Site of the third event in racing's triple crown, the Belmont Stakes, in June. Daily, May–July. (516)488-6000.

SALAMANCA

The largest reservation in New York is shaped like a crescent around Allegany State Park in a scenic mountain area. The Seneca were the most populous group in the Iroquois Confederacy, with territory extending from Lake Erie to the Finger Lakes. Like most of the Iroquois, the Seneca sided with Britain during the Revolution, and, as a result, were forced to cede most of their lands in 1797. Those who chose to remain in New York had more territory taken from them in a treaty signed illegally in 1838. Salamanca is the administrative center of the reservation.

 Seneca Nation Bingo. Sixty-five miles south of Buffalo, on U.S. 219. (716)945-1790.

SARATOGA SPRINGS

One of the most celebrated tracks in the United States. In continuous use since 1864, Saratoga's August meet is still the epitome of fashion and racing excitement. The resort first rose to prominence after the American Revolution because of its therapeutic waters. Their healing powers were known to the Mohawks and those traveling through the area were sure to take a dip in them for restorative purposes. The first resort in the area was built in 1802 and thirty years later the railroad began bringing the crowds from New York City. The first race track followed in the next decade. Saratoga Springs became the

Seneca-Iroquois National Museum

The Seneca were the Keepers of the Western Door in the Iroquois Confederacy. After the American Revolution, the door of history slammed shut on them. Troops who had ravaged their villages during the punitive Sullivan-Clinton raid in 1779 spread the word in the East about the fertility and beauty of the Iroquois land. With the coming of peace, they returned by the hundreds and their neighbors by the thousands. Many of the Seneca moved to Canada, and those who stayed were forced to relinquish their claim to the lands in the Big Tree Treaty of 1797.

A treaty made by the Seneca with Philadelphia financier Robert Morris, who in turn sold it to the Holland Company, allotted the tribe twelve parcels of land as reservations. Under the preemptive rights reserved to the buyers, however, these parcels were reduced to four in 1810. There followed a shameful period in which corrupt Seneca chiefs accepted payoffs from speculators for the remaining land. In 1842, state courts ruled that these agreements were nonbinding, and the tribe regained title to the land.

Because of all the land switches, Salamanca wound up as the only white town in America located in the middle of a reservation. The Seneca-Iroquois Museum is at the western edge of town, just off New York 17, on the Broad Street Extension, at the western Salamanca exit. It gives visitors a glimpse of this rich tribal history, with examples of wampum belts and various clan animals, and a sampling of both traditional and contemporary crafts. Open Monday–Saturday, 10–5; Sunday 12–5, May through September; closed Monday during the rest of the year. Suggested admission is a donation. For more information, call (716)945-1738. (From *North American Indian Landmarks: A Traveler's Guide,* by George Cantor, Visible Ink Press, 1993)

great resort of America's Gilded Age, where all the right people came to be seen. It started falling out of favor after the turn of the century, however, and continued to decline until the state stepped in during the 1930s with a restoration program for the springs. Another generation soon discovered the Victorian charm of the place and renovated several of the grand hotels and fine, summer homes. Now the Springs is once again a top resort, with facilities completely sold out during the August race meet.

Saratoga Race Course, thoroughbred track. On Union Avenue, east of Congress Park. Daily. (518)584-6200.

"DIAMONDS ARE FOREVER" AT THE TURNING STONE CASINO IN VERONA, NEW YORK. (COURTESY OF THE TURNING STONE CASINO)

VERONA

One of the smaller members of the Iroquois Confederacy, the Oneida were constantly replenishing their numbers by adopting captives taken in war. It is estimated that one-half of the tribe may have been brought in this way. The Oneida chose to scout for the Americans during the Revolution and were confirmed in their lands afterwards. However, the postwar onslaught of settlers convinced them to seek new territory in Wisconsin and the major part of the tribe left for the West in the 1820s. A remnant has stayed on in the Lake Oneida area.

 Turning Stone Casino, *(Oneida Nation of New York.)* Twenty miles west of Utica, at Exit 33 of the New York State Thruway. (315)361-7711.

YONKERS

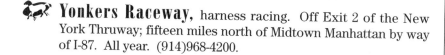 **Yonkers Raceway,** harness racing. Off Exit 2 of the New York Thruway; fifteen miles north of Midtown Manhattan by way of I-87. All year. (914)968-4200.

Pennsylvania

In Pennsylvania, gambling is limited to lottery tickets and placing bets at the track. For lottery information, contact the Pennsylvania State Lottery.

 Pennsylvania State Lottery, 2850 Turnpike Industrial Drive, Middletown 17057, (717)986-4699. Sales: $1.7 billion. Proceeds: $640 million. 100% senior citizens programs.

BENSALEM

 Philadelphia Park, thoroughbred track. North on Pennsylvania 132 and 513 from exit 25 of I-95, seventeen miles northeast of downtown Philadelphia. (215)639-9000.

GRANTVILLE

 Penn National, thoroughbred track. Off I-81 at the Grantville exit; eighteen miles northeast of downtown Harrisburg. All year. (717)469-2211.

WASHINGTON

 Ladbroke at the Meadows, harness racing. Off I-79 at Exit 8; twenty-four miles southwest of downtown Pittsburgh. All year. (412)225-9300.

WILKES-BARRE

 Pocono Downs, harness racing. East from Pennsylvania 309 on Pennsylvania 315. April–November. (717)825-6681.

28

SOUTHEAST

Alabama
Arkansas
Florida
Kentucky
Louisiana
Mississippi
North Carolina

Alabama
1. Creek Bingo Place, Atmore
2. Birmingham Race Track, Birmingham (closed)

Arkansas
3. Oaklawn Jockey Club, Hot Springs

Florida
4. Jai Alai, Dania
5. Jai Alai, Fort Pierce
6. Gulfstream Park, Hallandale
7. Hialeah Racetrack, Hialeah
8. Seminole Indian Bingo and Poker Casino, Hollywood
9. Seminole Gaming Palace, Immokalee
10. Calder Race Course, Miami
11. Miccosukee Indian Bingo and Gaming, Miami
12. Tampa Bay Downs, Oldsmar
13. Seminole Bingo of Brighton, Okechobee
14. Jai Alai, Orlando
15. Pompano Park, Pompano Beach
16. Jai Alai, Tampa
17. Seminole Gaming Palace of Tampa

Kentucky
18. Turfway Park, Florence
19. Ellis Park, Henderson
20. Keeneland Race Course, Lexington
21. Red Mile Harness Track, Lexington
22. Churchill Downs, Louisville

Louisiana
23. Belle of Baton Rouge
24. Casino Rouge, Baton Rouge
25. Horseshoe Casino and Hotel, Bossier City
26. Isle of Capri, Bossier City
27. Louisiana Downs, Bossier City
28. Cypress Bayou Casino, Charenton
29. Treasure Chest Casino, Kenner
30. Evangeline Downs, Lafayette
31. Grand Casino Avoyelles, Mansura
32. The Confederate Museum, New Orleans
33. The Contemporary Arts Center, New Orleans
34. The Historic New Orleans Collection, New Orleans
35. The Louisiana Nature and Science Center, New Orleans
36. The Louisiana State Museum, New Orleans
37. The New Orleans Historic Voodoo Museum, New Orleans
38. The New Orleans Museum of Art, New Orleans
39. The New Orleans Pharmacy Museum, New Orleans
40. The Wax Museum of Louisiana Legends, New Orleans
41. Bally's Belle of Orleans Casino, New Orleans
42. Flamingo Casino, New Orleans
43. Fair Grounds Race track, New Orleans
44. Harrah's Shreveport Casino, Shreveport
45. Delta Downs, Vinton

Mississippi
46. Casino Magic, Bay St. Louis
47. Boomtown Casino, Biloxi
48. Boomtown's Family Fun Center: The Motion Theater, Biloxi
49. Casino Magic, Biloxi
50. Grand Casino, Biloxi
51. Isle of Capri Casino, Biloxi
52. Treasure Bay Casino, Biloxi
53. Bayou Caddy's Jubilee Casino, Clermont Harbor
54. Copa Casino, Gulfport
55. Grand Casino Gulfport, Gulfport
56. Lady Luck Rhythm and Blues Casino, Lula
57. Lady Luck Natchez, Natchez
58. Silver Star Casino, Philadelphia
59. The Choctaw Indian Fair and Museum of the Southern Indian, Philadelphia
60. Bally's Saloon and Gambling Hall, Robinsonville
61. Circus Circus Casino, Robinsonville
62. Grand Casino Tunica, Robinsonville
63. Harrah's Casino Tunica, Robinsonville
64. Sam's Town Gambling Hall, Robinsonville
65. Sheraton Casino, Robinsonville
66. Ameristar Casino Vicksburg
67. Harrah's Casino & Hotel Vicksburg
68. Isle of Capri Casino, Vicksburg
69. Rainbow Casino, Vicksburg

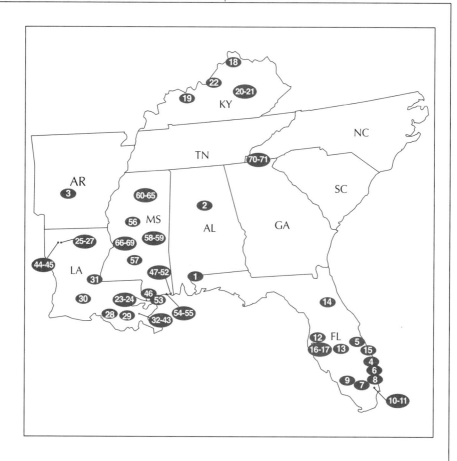

North Carolina

70. Cherokee Tribal Casino, Cherokee
71. The Museum of the Cherokee
   Indian, Cherokee

Alabama

The Poarch Band is a remnant of the mighty Creek Confederacy, the dominant tribe in Alabama until shattered by American forces at the Battle of Horseshoe Bend in 1814. This band managed to escape exile to Oklahoma twenty years later by hiding out in Florida. They later returned to live in agricultural communities, numbering about 600.

 Creek Bingo Palace *(Poarch Band of Creek Indians)*. Sixty miles northeast of Mobile by way of I-65 and Alabama 21. (334) 368-8007.

Arkansas

 Oaklawn Jockey Club, thoroughbred track. At 2705 Central Avenue. (Arkansas 7). Daily, February–April. (501) 623-4411.

Florida

Bingo, jai alai, greyhound racetracks, horse racing facilities, and ocean junket cruises are allowed by Florida law. Under present state legislature, casino gambling is not legal with the exception of some Indian gaming. For lottery information, contact the Florida State Lottery.

 Florida State Lottery, 250 Marriott Drive, Tallahassee 32301, (904)487-7777. Sales: $2.1 billion. Proceeds: $818 million. 100% Education.

DANIA

 Jai Alai is played at Dania Beach Boulevard (Florida A1A), east of U.S. 1; six miles south of Fort Lauderdale. Schedule varies, call in advance. (954)927-2841.

FORT PIERCE

 Jai Alai is played at 1750 S. Kings Highway (Florida 713); west of downtown, off I-95. December–April. (561)464-7500.

HALLANDALE

 Gulfstream Park, thoroughbred track. One of the leading Florida tracks. Home of the Florida Derby, Garden of Champions honors great throughbreds. U.S. 1 at Hallandale Beach Boulevard, south of Fort Lauderdale. Tuesday–Sunday, mid–January to March; Tuesday and Thursday–Sunday, April. (305)454-7000.

CAPTAIN BODGIT, LEFT, WINNER OF THE 1997 $500,000 FLORIDA DERBY, MAKES HIS MOVE IN TURN FOUR AT THE GULFSTREAM PARK RACE TRACK IN HALLENDALE, FLORIDA. (AP WIDE WORLD, GREGORY SMITH)

HIALEAH

 Hialeah Racetrack, thoroughbred track. 2200 E. Fourth Avenue, northwest of downtown Miami from the 79th Street NW exit of I-95. Legendary for the pink flamingos in the infield and the lush tropical landscaping of its grounds; an attraction in itself. Founder Joe Smoot imported the pink birds from Cuba when the track opened in 1931 as a way to establish an identity. He succeeded and the track's Flamingo Stakes is also one of the top events for three-year-olds. The track is open for tourists Monday–Friday, 9-5, when there is no racing. The meet runs March–May. (305)885-8000.

HOLLYWOOD

After fighting three wars against the United States, the Seminole were moved to four reservation tracts bordering the Everglades. They are a mixture of Southern tribes who fled south into Spanish Florida to escape attacks by the British and Americans in the late eighteenth and early nineteenth century. About two-thirds of the tribe now live in Oklahoma. The Florida group is composed of those who resisted exile and carried on the struggle from strongholds within the Glade. Never defeated and waging guerilla war against U.S. forces for decades, they finally made peace in 1858.

 Seminole Indian Bingo and Poker Casino. 4150 N. State Road 7, on the western edge of this northern suburb of Miami. (954)961-3220.

IMMOKALEE

This is an arm of the Big Cypress Seminole Reservation, on the northern edge of the Everglades.

 Seminole Gaming Palace. 506 S. First Street, thirty-six miles southeast of Fort Myers by way of Florida 82 and 29. (813)658-1313.

MIAMI

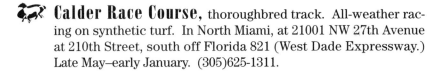 **Calder Race Course,** thoroughbred track. All-weather racing on synthetic turf. In North Miami, at 21001 NW 27th Avenue at 210th Street, south off Florida 821 (West Dade Expressway.) Late May–early January. (305)625-1311.

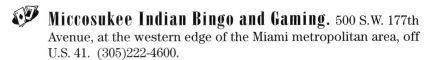 **Miccosukee Indian Bingo and Gaming.** 500 S.W. 177th Avenue, at the western edge of the Miami metropolitan area, off U.S. 41. (305)222-4600.

The Miccosukee branch of the Seminole speak a slightly different language than the rest of the tribe, indicating an origin from the Oconee tribe of Georgia. Their reservation is a 500-foot wide strip along five miles of the Tamiami Trail.

OLDSMAR

Tampa Bay Downs, thoroughbred track. The only track on Florida's Gulf Coast. Eleven miles northwest of Tampa, by way of westbound Florida 580 from I-275. Daily, early December–early May. (813)855-4401.

OKECHOBEE

 Seminole Bingo of Brighton. Southwest of Okechobee, by way of Florida 70 and County road 721, on the Brighton Seminole reservation. (305)792-1021.

ORLANDO

 Jai Alai is played in Fern Park, on U.S. 17, 192; eight miles north of downtown. All year. (407)339-6221.

POMPANO BEACH

 Pompano Park, harness racing. West from Pompano Beach exit of I-95 to Powerline Road. Daily, October–August. (954)972-2000.

TAMPA

 Jai Alai is played at South Dale Mabry Boulevard, just south of the Gandy Bridge; seven miles southwest of downtown. All year. (813)837-2441.

 Seminole Gaming Palace of Tampa. 5223 N. Orient Road, northern edge of the city. This facility is not on reservation land. (813)621-1302.

Kentucky

The state of Kentucky is synonymous with blue grass music and thoroughbred racing. For lottery information, contact the Kentucky State Lottery.

 Kentucky State Lottery, 6040 Dutchman's Lane, Louisville 40205, (502)473-2200. Sales: $543 million. Proceeds: $147 million. 100% General fund.

FLORENCE

 Turfway Park, thoroughbred track. Off exit 182 of I-75; eleven miles south of downtown Cincinnati, Ohio. Site of the Jim Beam Stakes, last Saturday in March, for three-year olds. Wednesday–Sunday, month of September and late November through March. (606)371-0200.

HENDERSON

 Ellis Park, thoroughbred track. North on U.S. 41, three miles south of downtown Evansville, Indiana. Tuesday–Sunday, late June–Labor Day, (502)826-0608.

LEXINGTON

Lexington is one of the prime historic sites of Kentucky thoroughbred racing. Sales at Keeneland, held five times annually, are the prime market for top American horses. Its library is regarded as the final word in documentation on thoroughbred lineage. The track itself is revered as the jewel box of American racing. The Blue Grass Stakes,

The Kentucky Derby Festival

For its first twenty-five years, the Kentucky Derby was regarded as little more than a regional event. When a master publicist, Matt Winn, took over management of Churchill Downs, it soon became a national phenomenon. Winn encouraged New York sportswriters to attend, and even paid their travel expenses, while showering them with thick Kentucky nostalgia and juleps. The stories they produced gave the Derby an aura, and the horses that entered its winner's circle went on to national prominence.

But Winn's big payoff came in 1915 when Regret, a filly owned by millionaire sportsman Harry Payne Whitney, came home a winner. Whitney's joy was unbounded and he called it "the greatest race in the world." From then on, the country pretty much agreed and Derby Day in Louisville grew into a media extravaganza. The weeks leading up to the big race have become a Kentucky original, with celebrations going on throughout the city. The race is now the first event in horseracing's Triple Crown, followed by the Preakness and Belmont Stakes races.

The Kentucky Derby Festival is a citywide celebration in Louisville, taking place the two weeks preceding the first Saturday in May. The Derby celebrates with "the world's largest fireworks show," a parade, a steamboat race on the Ohio River, a balloon race, concerts, entertainment, and the running of the Derby at Churchill Downs. For information, contact: The Kentucky Derby Festival, 137 W. Muhammad Ali Boulevard, Louisville, Kentucky 40202, (800)928-FEST. (from *Historic Festivals: A Traveler's Guide,* by George Cantor, Visible Ink Press, 1996)

held in April, is the last major race for three-year olds before the Kentucky Derby.

Keeneland Race Course, thoroughbred track. On U.S. 60, opposite the Blue Grass Airport, six miles west of downtown. The season runs for three weeks in April and three weeks in October. (606)254-3412.

Red Mile Harness Track. On Harrodsburg Rd. (U.S. 68), just southwest of central Lexington. The track is named for the color of the clay on the course and it is reputed to be the fastest in the world. Several world records for trotters and pacers have been set here. Wednesday–Saturday, late April–late June; Monday–Saturday, late September–mid October. (606)255-0752.

LOUISVILLE

An attraction in itself, this is the storied home of the Kentucky Derby, run the first Saturday in May. The track was founded in 1875, the same year the first Derby was run. Brilliant promotion and a series of stirring races in the World War I era turned the Derby from a sectional attraction to the best known horse race in the United States. A Derby museum is located adjacent to the track and is open daily, 9 a.m.-5 p.m.

 Churchill Downs, thoroughbred track, at 700 Central Avenue, north from I-264 at the Southern Parkway exit, or four miles south of downtown by way of Third Street. The meets here go from late April–June and late October–November. (502)636-4400.

Louisiana

Louisiana gaming laws permits both cruising and land-based riverboat casinos. Slots, blackjack, craps, video poker, and keno. For lottery information, contact the Louisiana State Lottery.

 Louisiana State Lottery, 11200 Industriplex Boulevard, Suite 150, Baton Rouge 70809. (504) 297-2000. Sales: $289 million. Proceeds: $102 million. 100% General fund.

BATON ROUGE

The Belle of Baton Rouge and the Casino Rouge are the only American riverboat casinos actually located in a state capital. But then veteran observers of Louisiana politics will tell you that Baton Rouge always has viewed its vices with a rather tolerant eye. Some of the nation's most powerful political machines were based here and few of them were noted for devotion to squeaky clean government. Combined with Louisiana's unique ambience, its mixture of Gallic and Hispanic ancestry that is unlike any other place in America, casinos seem to fit right in.

Memories of Huey Long survive at the skyscraper State Capitol. He built it and was buried in the gardens there after his assassination on its steps in 1935. Baton Rouge is also the home of Louisiana State University and Southern University, two institutions with especially scenic campuses. It is one of the busiest ports in the South, the head of the state's petrochemical industry. The city's relationship with the Mississippi River is explored at the Louisiana Naval War Memorial and the LASC Riverside Museum. Both are located in the downtown area between the two casinos.

Belle of Baton Rouge. The Belle is at 120 Front Street, exit 1A from I-110. Daily 10 a.m.–4 a.m. 719 slots, twenty-four black-

THE BELLE OF BATON ROUGE AT CATFISH TOWN. (COURTESY OF THE BELLE OF BATON ROUGE)

jack tables, five craps tables, eight poker tables. The Belle also offers caribbean stud poker, big six, video keno and video poker. (800) 266-2692.

Casino Rouge is located in the downtown area, further north of the Belle of Baton Rouge, at 1717 N. River Road, from the North Boulevard exit of I-100. Daily, twenty-four hours. (504) 381-7777.

BOSSIER CITY

The city grew up as an industrial suburb of Shreveport and is also the home of Barksdale Air Force Base. Oil refineries are the most notable landmarks in the area along the flats of the Red River.

Horseshoe Casino and Hotel. Take the first exit after the I-20 bridge across the Red River, 19-B, and follow signs to 711 Horseshoe Boulevard. Daily, twenty-four hours. 1060 slots, ninety-eight video poker machines, thirty-nine blackjack tables, eight craps tables, four roulette tables, twenty-one video keno machines, and baccarat. There are two restaurants and a lounge. (800) 895-0711.

CROWDS GATHER ON THE DECKS OF THE ISLE OF CAPRI TO VIEW THE CASINO MAGIC BOAT AS IT PASSES.
(AP WIDE WORLD, TOM STANFORD)

Isle of Capri. Leave I-20 and exit 20A, then south to 77 Hamilton Lane. Daily, twenty-four hours. (800) 386-4753.

Louisiana Downs, thoroughbred track. Across the Red River from downtown Shreveport, then east on U.S. 80 to I-220. July–November, with the main race being the Isle of Capri Super Derby in September. (318) 742-5555.

CHARENTON

A small group living in Bayou country, the Chitimacha first were overwhelmed militarily by the French and then culturally by the arrival of the Acadians into their homeland. Most have assimilated into the dominant Cajun culture and the last speakers of the Native language died out fifty years ago.

 Cypress Bayou Casino, *(Chitimacha Tribe).* 823 Martin Luther King Road, forty-five miles southeast of Lafayette by way of U.S. 90. (800) 284-4386.

KENNER

The Kenners were among the most prominent families in antebellum New Orleans. They owned sugar plantations and Duncan Kenner was appointed minister plenipotentiary to Europe by Jefferson Davis for the Confederate States. After the war, his property was confiscated but, eventually, he served on the U.S. Tariff Commission by appointment of President Arthur. The Kenner family built this town near their plantation in 1852 as an enticement for the railroad to extend its line their way. Tucked between the Mississippi River and Lake Ponchartrain, Kenner has several historic homes in the neighborhoods along the river and is also the home address of New Orleans International Airport.

 Treasure Chest Casino. Take the Williams Boulevard exit from I-10 and head north, to 5050 Williams Boulevard, on Lake Pontchartrain, thirteen miles northwest of central New Orleans. Daily, twenty-four hours. The Treasure Chest offers 854 slot machines, thirty blackjack tables, nine craps tables and three roulette tables. Video poker and Keno is also available. (504) 443-8000.

LAFAYETTE

Evangeline Downs, thoroughbred track. Three miles north on U.S. 167. Daily, May through Labor Day. (318) 896-7223.

MANSURA

Both Tunica and Biloxi tribes were driven out of Mississippi and came to live here. The Tunica originated in the Yazoo River Valley. They supported the French but were dispersed in tribal wars with other peoples in the area. The Biloxi controlled the Mississippi Gulf Coast when the French landed there. They, too, maintained friendly relations with France but when Britain took over the area after 1763 they were removed here.

 **Grand Casino Avoyelles,** *(Tunica-Biloxi Tribe).* Thirty-six miles southeast of Alexandria by way of Louisiana 1 and 114. (318) 253-9767.

NEW ORLEANS

New Orleans is one of the top tourism and entertainment centers in the United States. When Louisiana legalized riverboat gambling, casino operators could hardly wait to set up shop here. Instead, New Orleans was the site of one of the most spectacular failures in recent gaming history and has become a case study in the perils of assuming too much about the automatic success of casinos.

One of the licenses granted for New Orleans was given to Harrah's, a major player in the national casino business. It promised to build the world's largest casino in a prime, land-based location at the foot of

THE BALLY'S BELLE OF ORLEANS ON THE MISSISSIPPI. (AP WIDE WORLD, BURT STEEL)

Canal Street, within a short walk of the city's major hotels and the French Quarter. A temporary facility was opened in the former Municipal Auditorium, just across the street from the French Quarter. But the people never showed up. There are several theories about why they didn't. Some longtime residents feel that New Orleans symbolizes great food and jazz, and that is what the majority of visitors to the city want. They simply weren't interested in casinos. Others point out that the temporary casino was placed in an area perceived to be a high-crime district. Potential gamblers were leery about entering the area with large amounts of cash. Harrah's was forced to shut down the facility early in 1996 and declared bankruptcy. The partially finished casino on Canal Street was sealed while the state, city and corporation tried to figure out what to do next. As other large cities contemplate casinos, New Orleans has been studied repeatedly as an example of what can go wrong.

Even the more successful Flamingo has not operated without mishap. Late in 1996, a runaway barge on the Mississippi River crashed into the casino and adjacent Riverwalk shopping mall. There were several fatalities and the casino had to be shut down for several weeks.

Bally's Belle of Orleans Casino. Located at #1 Star Boulevard, the South Shore Harbor. Daily, twenty-four hours. (504)246-7777, (800)57-BALLY.

Museums in New Orleans

- The Confederate Museum (504)523-45222
- The Contemporary Arts Center (504)523-1216
- The Historic New Orleans Collection (504)523-4662
- The Louisiana Nature and Science Center (504)246-5672
- The Louisiana State Museum (504)568-6968
- The New Orleans Historic Voodoo Museum (504)523-7685
- The New Orleans Museum of Art (504)488-2631
- The New Orleans Pharmacy Museum (504)565-8027
- The Wax Museum of Louisiana Legends (504)525-2605, (800)233-5405

 Flamingo Casino. At The Riverwalk, the foot of Poydras Street, in the heart of downtown New Orleans, within walking distance of the historic French Quarter. Daily, twenty-four hours. 1318 slots, sixty-five blackjack tables, seven craps tables, four roulette tables, seven poker tables. The Flamingo also offers pai gow poker, baccarat, caribbean stud poker, big six, video keno and video blackjack. (504) 587-7777, (800)587-LUCK.

 Fair Grounds Race Track, thoroughbred track. Off Gentilly Boulevard, U.S. 90, just north of downtown. Venerable track where the mechanical starting gate was invented. Daily, Thanksgiving Day through March. (504) 944-5515.

SHREVEPORT

In the northwestern corner of the state, Shreveport traditionally looks to Texas for its economic and social bearings rather than the Cajun cities to its south. It is closely tied to the east Texas oil fields. They sent an initial wave of prosperity through the town in the early years of the twentieth century, making it Louisiana's second largest city.

The town is named for a steamboat builder, Henry M. Shreve. He was the first man to take a steamboat from Louisville to New Orleans and his improvements on Robert Fulton's original design won him navigational rights on the Mississippi. He was engaged by the U.S. Government in 1833 to break up a huge jam of driftwood, The Great Raft, which had accumulated over the centuries and blocked the Red River to navigation several miles below the present site of Shreveport. Using two battering ram vessels he designed for the purpose, Shreve cleared the river all the way into Oklahoma. He was one of the purchasers of the first land grant here in 1837 and the place was named for him two years later.

 Harrah's Shreveport Casino, at 315 Clyde Fant Parkway, along the riverfront, downtown. Daily, twenty-four hours. (318) 424-7777.

VINTON

 Delta Downs, thoroughbred track. Off I-10 at the Vinton exit; twenty-five miles west of Lake Charles. January–July. (318) 589-7441.

Mississippi

This state has permitted casino gaming to a wider extent than any other besides Nevada. Mississippi takes a free enterprise approach and has placed no set limit on the numbers. The law does stipulate, however, that casinos must be built on water to maintain the fiction that they are riverboats, unless the casino is owned by a Native American tribe, which allows for land-based casinos. The major concentrations are on the Gulf Coast and near the town of Tunica, on the Mississippi, just south of Memphis, Tennessee. In early 1997, there were a total of twenty-nine in the state. Slots, blackjack, craps, keno, video poker are all permitted. Mississippi's casinos are open daily, twenty-four hours.

BAY ST. LOUIS

This was a Gulf Coast resort for wealthy Delta planters as early as the 1820s. It was called Shieldsborough then after an early settler, but time and custom returned it to the name first given to these waters by the French explorer, Pierre d'Iberville, in 1699. It is now the western-most resort on the Mississippi Gulf Coast.

 Casino Magic, on Blue Meadow Road, off U.S. 90, fifty-five miles east of New Orleans, by way of I-10. There is a 201-room motor inn and a marina. 1,137 slots, twenty-eight blackjack tables, five craps tables, twelve poker tables, three roulette tables, three caribbean stud poker tables. Pai gow poker, baccarat, big six, keno and video keno are also available. (601) 466-0891.

BILOXI

It is unlikely that any area of the country underwent as complete a transformation in the last decade of the twentieth century as the Mis-

Boomtown's Family Fun Center: The Motion Theater

The Motion Theater creates a virtual reality experience by combining video, a state-of-the-art soundtrack and hydraulic motion seats. Participants can choose from a variety of experiences: Bobsled Ride; Cosmic Pinball; Four-Wheel Drive Truck; Mineshaft; Roller Coasters or a Run-Away Train. The Fun Center is open Sunday–Thursday 11 a.m. to 11 p.m. and Friday and Saturday 10 a.m. to 1 a.m.

sissippi Gulf Coast. In the 1980s, it was still a place of small motels, shrimp shacks on the pier, souvenir stands and one or two large resorts. But with the influx of gaming, the coast has developed one of the highest concentrations of casinos in America.

Most of the action is centered around Biloxi, the traditional heart of the resort beaches. The oldest European settlement in the state, it was the capital of France's colonial empire in the lower Mississippi Valley in the early eighteenth century. For generations, Biloxi had been a premier summer resort. Wealthy planters from all across the mid South, including Jefferson Davis, built summer estates on the ridge overlooking the Gulf. The pace of life was drowsy and full. Shipbuilding and shrimping were the bases of the town economy. As tastes in tourism began to change, a decline set in and the last of the grand resorts, the Broadwater, closed its doors. That event seemed to convince local leaders that casinos were the way to rebuild the tourist trade and the gaming proposal was passed easily in a local referendum.

Beach Boulevard remains a wide, oak-shaded thoroughfare along the shore. Most of the casinos are located here. Also on the boulevard are the Old Lighthouse, built in 1847, which legend says was painted black after Abraham Lincoln's assassination as a gesture of loyalty towards the restored Union. There is also Beauvoir, built in 1853 and the last home of the Confederate president, Davis. The J.J. Scott Marine Education Center has an aquarium with exhibits on the marine life in the area. Nearby are two vessels built as replicas of early twentieth century shrimp boats. That industry is also celebrated at the Maritime and Seafood Industry Museum, at the foot of the bridge to Ocean Springs.

 Boomtown Casino, located in the Back Bay area of town, off the Bayview Avenue exit of I-110. 955 slots, 181 video poker machines, twenty-four blackjack tables, four craps tables, two roulette tables, six poker tables. The Boomtown Casino also offers pai gow poker, caribbean stud poker, and video keno. (601) 435-7000.

Casino Magic, directly east of downtown, at 195 Beach Boulevard. Hotel accomodations available. 1210 slot machines including video poker, twenty-one blackjack tables, six craps tables, four roulette tables. Baccarat, pai gow poker, caribbean stud poker, big six, keno, video keno and video black jack is also available. (601) 562-4425, (800)5-MAGIC-5.

Grand Casino, east of town, on U.S. 90, at 265 Beach Boulevard. It is the largest of the Biloxi facilities, with an attached 490-room hotel and showroom. 1760 slots, ninety video poker machines, fifty-two blackjack tables, ten craps tables, six roulette tables, eighteen poker tables, twenty-four video keno machines, and twenty-four keno seats. The Grand Casino also offers baccarat, pai gow poker, caribbean stud poker, and big six. (601) 435-8930, (800)WIN-2-WIN.

Isle of Capri Casino, located on U.S. 90, east of town. This 370-room hotel on the Gulf has an indoor twenty-five foot waterfall, palm trees, rock formations, a simulated thunderstorm, and a talking parrot. The Isle also offers live entertainment in the atrium. 1,125 slots, eight poker tables, thirty-one blackjack tables, four craps tables. Big six, caribbean stud poker, let it ride, mini-baccarat, pai gow poker and roulette tables are also available. (601) 435-5400, (800)THE-ISLE.

Treasure Bay Casino, located west of town on U.S. 90, at 1980 Beach Boulevard. Hotel. (800) PIRATE-9.

CLERMONT HARBOR

This is an area long favored by wealthy New Orleans families as a summer resort. It is close enough to the city to allow businessmen to commute. It first rose to favor in the nineteenth century as an escape from the yellow fever epidemics that ravaged the city in the hot weather but later developed as a pleasure resort.

Bayou Caddy's Jubilee Casino. From the Mississippi 607 exit of I-10, then east on U.S. 90 to 5005 S. Beach Boulevard. Fifty miles east of New Orleans, by way of U.S. 90. (800) 552-0707.

GULFPORT

Unlike the other communities on Mississippi's Gulf Coast, this is a planned city, built by a railroad as a port for shipping pine wood and later cotton. Gulfport was built starting in 1902 to take advantage of the best natural harbor on the coast. Work was initiated by Gulf and Ship Island Railroad, which was later acquired by the Illinois Central. Only when the timber stands were depleted did Gulfport begin to develop its recreational facilities. It still bears the look of a working town rather than a resort, but it features excellent deep water fishing excursions and is the point of departure to Ship Island, part of the Gulf Islands National Seashore with impressive Civil War military installations. The Marine Life Oceanarium features dolphin and sea lion shows, bird shows, a touch pool in Aqua Stadium, underwater dive shows, and a twenty-five minute train tour to Gulfport's Small Craft Harbor. Call (601)863-0651 for hours and ticket information.

Copa Casino. The Copa, a former Caribbean cruise ship with nine decks, is berthed in the port area, south of the junction of U.S. 90 and 49, at 777 Copa Boulevard. 700 slots, fifteen video poker machines, nineteen blackjack tables, four poker tables, in addition to big six, caribbean stud poker, let it ride, and roulette. (601) 863-3330, (800)WIN-COPA.

Grand Casino Gulfport. Grand Casino is just west of downtown, at 3215 W. Beach Boulevard. The hotel with 407 rooms overlooking the Gulf also offers six restaurants: Fifty Fifties Food Court, Banana's—The Ultimate Buffet, Side Street Bar-B-Q n' Blues Cafe, The Crab House, The Liberty Grill, and Magrolsa's Casual Dining. The America Live Party Barge features live entertainment, bars and lounges. 1,766 slots, 246 poker machines, fifty blackjack tables, six roulette tables, fourteen poker tables, twenty-four keno seats, twenty-four video keno machines, sixty video blackjack machines, four caribbean stud poker tables, eight craps tables. (601) 435-8930, (800)946-7777.

LULA

Just a few miles from the traditional Delta blues crossroads (the junction of U.S. 49 and 61), Lula has built its casino around a musical theme. Nearby Moon Lake is a longtime resort in the area. It was the scene of a failed attempt by U.S. Grant to dynamite a passage from the Mississippi to inland streams so he could attack Vicksburg from the rear in 1863.

Lady Luck Rhythm and Blues Casino. On U.S. 49, directly across the Mississippi River bridge from Helena, Arkansas. Seventy miles south of Memphis. Motor inn with 173 rooms. (800) 789-5825.

NATCHEZ

The historic jewel of the mid-South, Natchez is a dream of antebellum glory. The fortunes made in cotton were spent here to build one of the most stunning groups of stately homes in America. Pillared and vast, the homes of Natchez are the romantic image of what the Old South was like. The Spring Pilgrimage, during which most of them are open to the public, is among the best attended historic travel events on the calendar.

Natchez grew up during the great era of the flatboats, in the early years of the nineteenth century. It was a traditional stopover before the final push to New Orleans. Even more important, it was where the boatmen gathered to start the long, land trek home over the Natchez Trace, the road that ran to Nashville, Tennessee. The Trace brought the wealth of the Mississippi Valley flowing through the community and much of it stayed.

After statehood was attained in 1817, the city became the center of the Delta's cotton kingdom, a gracious fantasy built upon the backs of brutal slave labor. It was occupied by Union forces in 1863 and time seems to have stopped since then. Natchez never regained its economic importance, but that also insured that what had been built here would not be replaced. A few of the mansions are open year-round and several of them have been turned into bed-and-breakfasts.

Under-the-Hill was the place where the steamboats landed. It was a rowdy precinct, where well-bred ladies never ventured. The tough boatmen, many of whom were pirates when the opportunity presented itself, mingled with thieves of every description and the area was a haven of prostitution and gambling. Under-the-Hill has cleaned up quite a bit since then, however, and it is here that the riverboat casino is docked.

 Lady Luck Natchez. In the Under-the-Hill district on the riverfront, at 70 Silver Street. Daily, twenty-four hours. (800) 722-5825.

PHILADELPHIA

The most prosperous and powerful Native group in Mississippi, the Choctaw were a highly-advanced agricultural society. They consis-

The Choctaw Indian Fair and Museum of the Southern Indian

The Museum of the Southern Indian is located in the Pearl River Community, which is immediately east of Philadelphia. The annual fair is held here also. The museum gives a historical overview of the development of the tribe. During the Choctaw Fair, there is traditional dancing and pageantry, including hotly contested stickball games. Admission to the museum is free, and it is open Monday–Friday, 8 a.m.–4:30 p.m. The four-day Choctaw Fair begins on the Wednesday following the Fourth of July. For more information, call (601)656-5251.

tently allied themselves with the European powers during the colonial period. But when white settlers came pouring into their lands after Mississippi attained statehood the record didn't help them at all. Forced to cede their territory, the Choctaw were removed to Oklahoma in the 1830s. About one-quarter of the tribe managed to stay behind and in recent years it has developed a strong cultural identification. The annual Choctaw Indian Fair in Philadelphia is the best-attended such event in the Eastern United States.

 Silver Star Casino, *(Mississippi Band of Choctaw).* Highway 16 West, forty miles northwest of Meridian. (601) 650-1234.

ROBINSONVILLE

Commentators agree that by most measures of poverty Tunica County came in last in the United States. Chronically depressed, it was an area of small sharecroppers struggling to scrape a living out of the black Delta soil. Just beyond the reach of suburban Memphis, it was a vision that America preferred not to see, a permanent peasant class bound to the land.

But that was before the casinos came. Tunica now has the South's largest concentration of gaming and it has been transformed into an entertainment center. Stars of blues and country music perform nightly in the glittering casinos. While its supporters claim that Tunica has risen fast on the quality of life charts, gaming opponents argue that much of that gain is based on the fact that many of its poorest inhabitants can no longer afford to live there because of the soaring property values. The casinos have also turned Memphis into the fourth-largest metropolitan feeder area for gaming—after New York, Philadelphia and Los Angeles.

The casinos are clustered near what was once the town of Commerce. All the casinos are located on Mississippi 304, west of U.S. 61, thirty miles south of Memphis. For a brief time it was a rival to Memphis for the steamboat trade. But the river swallowed it whole in the 1850s before levees could be put in place, and the area's only fling with prosperity ended. Until the casinos arrived.

Bally's Saloon and Gambing Hall, two-and-a-half miles west of U.S. 61. Daily, twenty-four hours. 238-room hotel. 1,100 slots, eighty-two video poker machines, forty-four blackjack tables, eight craps tables, four caribbean stud poker tables. Also offers poker, roulette, big six, and other special gaming machines. Nightclub. (800) 382-2559.

Circus Circus Casino, with its family-themed entertainment, is open daily, twenty-four hours. 1,369 slots, ninety-one video poker machines, forty-one blackjack tables, nine craps tables, four roulette tables, six poker tables, ten video keno machines, and three caribbean stud poker tables. Guest can also enjoy three restaurants: The Big Top Buffet, JoJo's Cafe & Ice Cream Parlour and The Amazing Linguini Brothers; and two lounges: The Band Wagon Bar & Stage and The Amazing Linguini Brothers Bar. (601) 357-1183, (800)9-CIRCUS.

Grand Casino Tunica, claims to have the largest gaming area of any casino between Las Vegas and Atlantic City. Opened in 1996. 188-room hotel. (601) 357-3193.

Harrah's Casino Tunica, is situated on a triple-decked barge and has live entertainment on weekends. 200-room hotel. (601) 363-7200.

Sam's Town Gambling Hall, is housed within a replica of a nineteenth century main street area. In an area the size of two football fields, guests can enjoy gambling with twenty times the odds, single deck 21, and table limits of up to $5,000. 1,621 slots, 153 video poker machines, forty-two blackjack tables, ten craps tables, four roulette tables, twelve poker tables, seven caribbean stud poker tables, fifty-five keno seats, twenty video keno machines. Baccarat, pai gow poker, big six, and video blackjack are also available. Sam's Town offers a number of dining choices: Billy Bob's Steakhouse & Saloon, Corky's Bar-B-Q, Smokey Joe's Cafe & Market, the Uptown Buffet and Calamity Jane's Ice Cream Parlor & Coca Cola Museum. There is live music in three auditoriums. The 506-room hotel, includes such amenities as a gazebo, Jacuzzi, sauna, pool, a poolside snack bar, workout room, and room service. (800) 456-0711.

 Sheraton Casino, opened in early 1997 and is the most recent addition to the casino area. Hotel with 513 rooms. Luxury touches in the pool and spa areas. (800) 391-3777.

VICKSBURG

Vicksburg's name is ineradicably linked with a turning point of the Civil War. Just as in Gettysburg, Pennsylvania, with whom it shares the date of battle, the rest of Vicksburg's past is overshadowed by the events of July 3, 1863. On that date, the city surrendered to the besieging forces of U.S. Grant after forty-seven days. Full control of the Mississippi River passed to the Union side, cutting the Confederacy apart and making the final result inevitable.

The city's history began, however, in 1814 when a Methodist minister, Rev. Newitt Vick, opened a mission here. As the river commerce flowed past its door, the mission became a town and then one of the most important cities in the state in the antebellum years. An economic powerhouse in Mississippi's cotton economy, Vicksburg rivaled Natchez as a center of culture and political power. After the war, they also shared a decline. Vicksburg's was almost fatal. The Mississippi changed its course during the floods of 1876 and the former port city was left without an outlet to the river. But a federal projected diverted the waters of the Yazoo River to form a canal and regained Vicksburg's port in 1902.

Vicksburg has a wealth of restored homes in its historic district, some of which still show the scars of battle. The National Military Park adjoins the city on the north and east and furnishes an invaluable lesson in the trench warfare that Grant came to master. The Waterways Experiment Station is a research lab of the U.S. Army Corps of Engineers and shows fascinating exhibits on flood control and how wild rivers are managed.

The casinos in downtown Vicksburg are reached from exit 1A of I-20, the first Misisippi exit across the Mississippi River bridge, and then north.

 Ameristar Casino Vicksburg is at 4146 S. Washington Street. The Ameristar is modeled after the historic riverboats of the 1870s, and is the largest casino in central Mississippi, with 84,000 square-feet. Nationally know headliners entertain guests in the 450-seat Delta Grand Showroom. The Cabaret Lounge also features top show groups every night. 871 slots, fifty-five video poker machines, forty blackjack tables, six craps tables, seven poker tables, four caribbean stud poker tables, seven video keno machines, and seven video blackjack machines. Daily, twenty-four hours. (601)638-1000, (800)700-7770.

Harrah's Casino & Hotel Vicksburg is at 1310 Mulberry Street. Daily, twenty-four hours. Hotel with 117 rooms. (800) 843-2343.

Isle of Capri Casino is at 3990 Washington Street. Caribbean theme. Hotel. 692 slot machines, fifty poker machines, twenty-six blackjack machines, five craps machines, seven poker tables, six video keno machines, and four video blackjack machines. Roulette, baccarat, caribbean stud poker, and big six games are also available. Daily, twenty-four hours. (601) 636-5700, (800)THE-ISLE.

Rainbow Casino at Vicksburg Landing is situated on a barge, at 1440 Warrenton Road. Daily, twenty-four hours. (800) 503-3777.

North Carolina

CHEROKEE

This group of Cherokee represents those who succesfully hid in the mountains from American forces sent to remove them to Oklahoma on the Trail of Tears in the 1830s. The most assimilated and economically successful of all tribes, the Cherokee thought Congress would protect their land rights. But President Andrew Jackson, ignoring rulings by the U.S. Supreme Court, ordered the Cherokee removed from their historic homes in Tennessee and Georgia. The federal government eventually recognized the determination of the eastern Cherokee and established reservation lands for them here. Capitalizing on their proximity to a vast tourist area and a national park, the Cherokee have built up one of the most profitable tourism operations among Native Americans, with museums, craft shops and a theater as part of the mix.

 Cherokee Tribal Casino, *(Eastern Band of Cherokee).* At the southern entrance to Great Smoky Mountains National Park, on U.S. 441. (704) 497-6835.

The Museum of the Cherokee Indian

In place of the living approach, the museum takes a decidedly modern approach. Extensive collections of tribal artifacts, clothing, and crafts are presented within the framework of their historical and cultural contexts, supplemented by an impressive range of audio and video tapes. Six mini-theaters offer presentations about prehistoric through modern times. "Hear-phones" allow visitors to listen to ancient legends in the Cherokee language; a display illuminates each written character of the Sequoyan syllabary (which has preserved the language in written form since 1821) as is is pronounced, so that visitors may learn about the language while hearing it spoken. A presentation in the museum's auditorium provides an inside glimpse into the present-day Cherokee community.

Location: North on U.S. 441.

Hours: September—mid-June: Daily, 9 a.m.—5 p.m. Mid-June—late August: Monday—Saturday, 9 a.m.—8 p.m., and Sunday, 9 a.m.—5:30 p.m.

Admission: $4.00, children ages six—twelve, $2.00, children under age five are admitted for free.

For More Information: (704)497-3481

(From *North American Indian Landmarks: A Traveler's Guide*, by George Cantor, Visible Ink Press, 1993)

GREAT LAKES & OHIO VALLEY

Illinois
Indiana
Michigan
Minnesota
West Virginia
Wisconsin

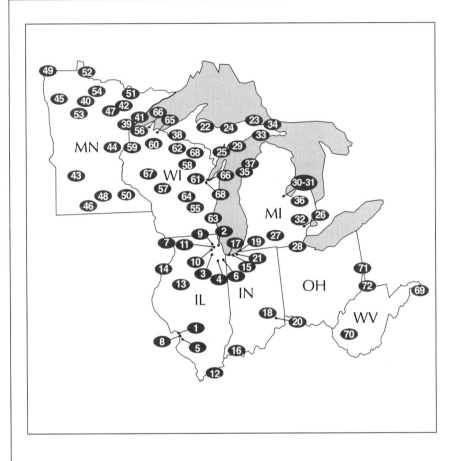

Illinois

1. Alton Belle Riverboat Casino, Alton
2. Arlington International Racecourse, Arlington Heights (closed)
3. Hollywood Casino, Aurora
4. Hawthorne Race Course and Sportsman's Park, Cicero
5. Fairmount Park, Collinsville
6. Balmoral Park, Crete
7. Silver Eagle, East Dubuque
8. Casino Queen, East St. Louis
9. Grand Victoria Casin, Elgin
10. Empress Casino Joliet, Joliet
11. Maywood Park, Maywood
12. Players Casino, Metropolis
13. Par-a-dice Riverboat Casino, Peoria
14. Jumer's Casino Rock Island, Rock Island

Indiana

15. Showboat Mardi Gras Casino, East Chicago
16. Casino Aztar, Evansville
17. Majestic Star and Trump Casino, Gary
18. Empress Casino, Hammond
19. Argosy Casino, Lawrenceburg
20. Blue Chip Casino, Michigan City
21. Grand Victoria Casino and Hyatt Resort, Rising Sun

Michigan

22. Ojibwa Casino, Baraga
23. Bay Mills Resort and Casino, Brimley
24. Christmas Kewadin Casino, Christmas
25. Chip-In Casino, Harris

26. Hazel Park Harness Raceway, Hazel Park
27. Jackson Harness Raceway, Jackson
28. Ladbroke Detroit Race Course, Livonia
29. Manistique Kewadin, Manastique
30. Mt. Pleasant Meadows, Mt. Pleasant
31. Soaring Eagle Casino, Mt. Pleasant
32. Northville Downs, Northville
33. Kewading Shores Casino, St. Ignace
34. Vegas Kewadin Casino, Sault Ste. Marie
35. Leelenau Sands Casino, Suttons Bay
36. Sports Creek Raceway, Swartz Creek
37. Turtle Creek Casino, Traverse City
38. Lac Vieux Desert Casino, Watersmeet

Minnesota

39. Black Bear Casino, Carlton
40. Che-We Casino and Palace Casino, Cass Lake
41. Fond du Luth Casino, Duluth
42. Grand Portage Casino, Grand Portage
43. Firefly Creek Casino, Granite Falls
44. Grand Casino Hinckley, Hinckley
45. Shooting Star Casino, Mahnomen
46. Jackpot Junction, Morton
47. Grand Casino Mille Lacs, Onamia
48. Little 6 Bingo, Prior Lake
49. Red Lake Casino, Red Lake

50. Treasure Island Casino, Red Wing
51. River Road Casino, Thief River Falls
52. Fortune Bay Casino, Tower
53. Northern Lights Casino, Walker
54. Lake of the Woods Casino, Warroad

Wisconsin

55. Hochunk Casino, Baraboo
56. Isle Vista Casino, Bayfield
57. Majestic Pines Casino, Black River Falls
58. Mohican North Star Casino, Bowler
59. Hole in the Wall Casino, Danbury
60. Lac Courte Oreilles Casino, Hayward
61. Menominee Nation Casino, Keshena
62. Lake of the Torches Casino, Lac du Flambeau
63. Potawatomi Bingo, Milwaukee
64. Rainbow Casino, Nekoosa
65. Bad River Casino, Odanah
66. Oneida Bingo, Oneida
67. St. Croix Casino, Turtle Lake
68. Northern Lights Casino, Wabeno

West Virginia

69. Charles Town Races, Charles Town
70. Tri-State Greyhound Track, Charleston
71. Mountaineer Race Track and Resort, Chester
72. Wheeling Downs, Wheeling

Illinois

Riverboat gambling became legal in the state on January 1, 1991. While the Gaming Board of Illinois does not mandate wagering limits, it does require the riverboat cruises to last no longer than four hours. To obtain lottery information, contact the Illinois State Lottery.

 Illinois State Lottery, 676 N. Street Clair, Chicago 60611, (312)793-3026. Sales: $1.6 billion. Proceeds: $594. 100% education.

ALTON

Alton rivaled St. Louis as a Mississippi River steamboat port in the mid-nineteenth century. Situated on a high bluff just north of the junction with the Missouri River, the place was destined by geography to play a major role in the river economy. South of here, the Illinois bank flattens out and is the site of industrial installations. Since Alton is the last landing place before the start of bluff country, it was a natural location for a port.

The city was formed by merging three communities, the largest of which was founded by Col. Rufus Easton in 1816 and named for his son. Because of its location across from a slaveholding state, Alton was chosen by abolitionist editor Elijah Lovejoy as the base for his publication. He was murdered here by a pro-slavery mob in 1837. A Confederate prison stood here during the war and the remains of its walls can be seen at Broadway and William. Alton is also known for its antique shops, located between George and State Streets in the historic district.

Alton Belle Riverboat Casino, at 219 Piasa Street. Daily, 7 a.m.–3 a.m. Boarding every thirty minutes. Twenty-two miles north of downtown St. Louis, Missouri, by way of I-70, Missouri 367 and U.S. 67. (800)336-7568.

THE ALTON BELLE RIVERBOAT CASINO. (COURTESY OF THE ALTON BELLE RIVERBOAT CASINO)

ARLINGTON HEIGHTS

 Arlington International Racecourse, thoroughbred track. East of the Euclid Avenue exit of I-280 and Illinois 53, northwest suburbs of Chicago. Closed in September, 1997.

AURORA

Aurora grew up as two intensely antagonistic communities on either side of the Fox River. They made peace and merged only when it was agreed to place the city hall on an island in midstream. Aurora was founded in 1834 on the site of a Potawatomi village and grew up as a manufacturing and rail town, slightly outside the Chicago suburban orbit. It originally intended to call itself Wabonsie, after a local Native American leader. But when it was learned that another Illinois town had beaten them to it, town leaders decided on Aurora, or dawn, as a classical equivalent to the meaning of the chief's name in English.

Hollywood Casino, at 1 New York Street Bridge. Daily, twenty-four hours. Thirty-nine miles west of downtown Chicago, by way of I-290 and 88. (630)801-1234.

CICERO

 Hawthorne Race Course and Sportsman's Park, thoroughbred track. These adjoining tracks are on South Laramie, north of Illinois 50 from I-55, southwest of central Chicago. Both tracks are open Monday to Saturday. Hawthorne's season runs from early October–December. (708)780-3700. They run at Sportsman's Park, from mid-February to early May. (773)242-1121.

COLLINSVILLE

 Fairmount Park, thoroughbred track. At I-255 and Collinsville Road, eleven miles east of downtown St. Louis, Missouri, by way of I-55 and I-255. Monday to Saturday, mid-March to early November. (314)436-1516.

CRETE

 Balmoral Park, harness racing. On Illinois 1, at 26435 S. Dixie Highway; thirty-six miles south of Chicago by way of I-94 and Illinois 394. Monday to Saturday, year-round. (708)672-7544.

EAST DUBUQUE

The town grew up as a ferryboat landing and rail transfer point for its larger neighbor on the west bank of the Mississippi River.

 Silver Eagle, berthed at the Frentress Lake Marina, on U.S. 20. Hour-long cruises depart 9:30 a.m.–4:30 p.m. Across the river from Dubuque, Iowa. (815)747-2455.

EAST ST. LOUIS

This is one of the legendary border towns in American history. The accommodating leaders of East St. Louis permitted the sort of activities that were outlawed in the metropolis across the river. Duke Ellington's famous "East St. Louis Toddle-oo," for many years the theme music of his band, was written as a tribute to the easy-going lifestyle.

The town grew out of the historic French fur-trading outpost of Cahokia. It then became the great trans-shipment point to the West, as cargoes were unloaded and warehoused here for ferrying across the river. It was originally known as Illinoistown, but when

THE CASINO QUEEN RIVERBOAT SITS ON THE MISSISSIPPI RIVERFRONT OF EAST ST. LOUIS, ILLINOIS. (AP WIDE WORLD, ODELL MITCHELL JR.)

several communities merged in 1861, the new name was adopted. By 1900, it had one of the largest black populations of any city in Illinois and was the scene of racial rioting during World War I. East St. Louis in its heyday was an industrial giant but since the 1950s has fallen victim to urban blight. However, the casino is fully in keeping with its colorful past.

Casino Queen, Across from St. Louis, Missouri and the Gateway Arch, at 200 S. Front Street. (618)874-5000, (800)777-0777. Two-hour cruises depart 9 a.m.–5 a.m. Offers 944 slots, forty-six blackjack tables, eight craps tables, four roulette tables, eighteen video keno machines.

ELGIN

The watches that once made the name of this town famous throughout the country are no longer made here. In its time, however, the Elgin factory was regarded as a marvel, introducing assembly line techniques as early as 1872. Elgin was also a center of the dairy industry and it was here that Gail Borden perfected the process for condensed milk. The town is situated on both banks of the Fox River.

Grand Victoria Casino, at 250 S. Grove Avenue. 9 a.m.–3 a.m. Sunday to Thursday; open to 5 a.m. on Friday and Saturday. Forty-two miles northwest of Chicago by way of I-90. (847)695-7540.

Massac State Park

Massac State Park in Metropolis, is Illinois' first state park. With 1,450 acres, visitors can enjoy camping, boating, hiking, fishing, hunting, and horseback riding. The park features a reconstructed timber fort originally built in 1794. During the month of October and certain weekends through-out the year, visitors can experience what life was like during the 1700s. Food, crafts, costumes and battle reenactments make the experience more realistic. Contact the park office for more information, (618)524-4712.

JOLIET

The city was laid out along the river but didn't start to thrive until the Illinois and Michigan Canal was completed in 1848. The waterway connected Lake Michigan with the Mississippi River and gave Joliet a market for its locally quarried limestone and, later, its manufactured products. There is evidence that its settlers were lovers of Shakespeare and intended to call the place Juliet. There is, indeed, a Romeoville just a few miles north. But later residents preferred the name of the French explorer, Louis Joliet, who came through the area in 1673.

Joliet is also famous in the annals of crime as the site of the state penitentiary to which some of the more notorious figures in Chicago's history were sent.

Empress Casino Joliet, west of downtown at I-55, exit 248. The Empress I operates from 7 a.m.–midnight; Empress II from 11 a.m.–2:45 a.m. (708)345-6789.

Harrah's Casino. Downtown, on Joliet Street, at the Des Plaines River. the Northern Star, 10:30 a.m.–1:30 a.m. The Northern Star is a 210-foot yacht, offering 400 slots. Southern Star II operates 9 a.m.–5 a.m. The Southern Star is a 210-foot traditional paddlewheeler and offers 495 slots. The following table games are available on both boats: blackjack, caribbean stud poker, craps, mini–bacarrat and roulette. Harrah's Landing in the Pavilion features live entertainment, a gift shop and fine dining. (800)427-7247.

MAYWOOD

 Maywood Park, harness racing. At North and Fifth Avenues., north from exit 20 of the Eisenhower Freeway (I-290); fiteen miles

PLAYERS CASINO, MOORED AT MERV GRIFFIN'S RIVERBOAT LANDING ON THE OHIO RIVER, LIGHTS UP THE NIGHT IN METROPOLIS, ILLINOIS. (AP WIDE WORLD, ELIZABETH COURTNEY)

west of downtown Chicago. February–May, October–December. (708)343-4800.

METROPOLIS

This old Ohio River port, built near an eighteenth century French outpost, was a deservedly obscure sort of place until the 1930s. With the publication of the instantly popular Superman comic books, set in a fictional city called Metropolis, the Illinois namesake suddenly became famous. Although it shares almost nothing with the haunt of Clark Kent and Lois Lane, Metropolis began attracting a few curious tourists. In the 1970s, it decided to start cashing in on the association. It now holds an annual Superman Festival in June and a new Super Museum contains memorabilia of the hero's life in comics, television and the movies.

Metropolis was given its hopeful name by founder William McBane. He thought it would be the site of an Ohio River bridge which would turn it into the leading city of the West. That didn't happen. Fort Massac State Park, just east of town, preserves the site of the French frontier post, built in 1757 and used by George Rogers Clark during the Revolutionary War.

Players Casino. On Front Street at the Ohio River landing. Saturday to Thursday, 9 a.m.–1 a.m.; open to 3 a.m. on Friday and Saturday. Twelve miles west of Paducah, Kentucky, on I-24. (618)524-5518. Offers 850 slots, ninety-four video poker machines, thirty-five blackjack tables, six craps tables, five roulette tables, eight video keno machines.

PEORIA

This is one of the great river cities in Illinois history. Located on the main route of exploration from the Great Lakes to the Mississippi Valley, it was visited in the late seventeenth century by Louis Joliet, Fr. Jacques Marquette and Robert LaSalle. It claims to have been the first European settlement in the state, with evidence for a French presence here as early as 1691. The Illinois River turned Peoria into the state's second largest city (it now has fallen to third) for almost a century. The city still celebrates a Steamboat on the Riverfront Festival every June.

 Par-a-dice Riverboat Casino. On the riverfront in East Peoria. (800)727-2342. Boarding every three hours, 9 a.m.–midnight. 872 slots, 104 video poker machines, twenty-seven blackjack tables, four craps tables, three roulette tables, twelve video keno machines. Guests can enjoy dining in the Boulevard Grille, the Grandview Room and the Broadway Buffet. The Par-a-Dice Riverboat Casino is 238-feet long and has four decks.

ROCK ISLAND

Where the Rock River flows into the Mississippi was an important strategic point to both Native Americans and the white settlers who followed on their lands. This was the home of Black Hawk, the great Sac & Fox leader, who led the final, futile resistance in the 1830s. A state park memorializes one of his lookout points on the bluffs above the city. Rock Island rose to greater military prominence during the Civil War when it was selected as the site of the U.S. Army's largest arsenal. The Rock Island Arsenal is still active on its island in the Mississippi and a museum traces the history of the weapons that were made here. There is also an observation deck that enables visitors to watch one of the river's huge navigational locks in action.

There are three casino riverboats in the Quad Cities area, but this is the only one on the Illinois side of the river.

Jumer's Casino Rock Island, at 18th Street and the riverfront. Sunday to Thursday, 9 a.m.–11 p.m.; Friday and Saturday, open to 1 a.m. Boarding every two hours. (800)477-7747.

Indiana

Laws governing the operation of the Indiana riverboat casinos are essentially the same as Illinois'. The casinos are land-based but can only be entered, or boarded, at stipulated times to carry on the legal fiction that they are actual riverboats. The riverboats offer the full range of casino games, including slots, craps, blackjack, and roulette. Lottery information can be obtained by contacting the Indiana State Lottery.

 Indiana State Lottery, 201 S. Capitol Avenue, Suite 1100, Indianapolis 46225, (317)264-4800. Sales: $621 million. Proceeds: $187 million. 100% general fund.

EAST CHICAGO

One of the great manufacturing cities of the Calumet district, East Chicago was the home of Inland Steel and Youngstown Sheet and Tube. Indiana Harbor, created in 1903 on the town's Lake Michigan shoreline, turned a quiet lakeside community into an industrial giant. Much of that muscle now lies slack, and the casino occupies what was once a booming industrial area.

 Showboat Mardi Gras Casino. Twenty-two miles southeast of Chicago at the Donald Marina on Indiana Harbor, by way of the Cline Avenue exit from I-90, the Chicago Skyway. (219)391-7777. Daily, twenty-four hours, with boarding at two-hour intervals.

EVANSVILLE

This is the largest city on the Ohio River west of Louisville. Evansville, named for one of its early sponsors, rose to prosperity dur-

ing the years of flatboat commerce. Situated on a huge U-curve of the river, it contains a wealth of mid-nineteenth century public and commercial buildings. Most date from the city's gilded era and many of them lie on the Downtown Walkway, a pedestrian path along the former Main Street. Evansville also marks its association with the waterway in the Ohio River Festival of the Arts, on the second weekend of May. Powerboat races are held on the river in late June.

In the Evansville Museum of Arts and Science is Rivertown USA, a reproduction of a typical nineteenth century river community.

Casino Aztar. 700 NW Riverside Drive. Daily, 9 a.m.–5 a.m. (812)433-4000.

GARY

These side-by-side casinos share a site on the Lake Michigan shore, amid Gary's industrial complex. This was a twentieth century boomtown, created by the chairman of U.S. Steel Corp., Judge Elbert Gary. First proposed in the corporation's annual report in 1905, Gary became a reality by the end of the decade, a city built from scratch amid the dunes and grass of an uninhabited stretch of lakeshore. By 1920 it was one of Indiana's largest cities and won everlasting fame in the 50s when it figured in a song title and pivotal plot device in the musical hit "The Music Man."

Always a polyglot community, with one of the largest foreign-born populations in the country, Gary also drew from the internal migration of African Americans from the South. It became one of the first large cities to elect a black mayor in the 1960s and remains a place with a strong black political establishment. Wounded severely by the decline of domestic steel production, Gary turned to casinos as a brake upon economic decline. The city celebrates a Lakefront Festival on June 1.

Majestic Star and Trump Casino. The two casinos, although separately operated, are connected by an interior passage. They are located at Buffington Harbor, west of downtown, at the Indiana 912 exit of I-90. Cruises board every two hours, 8 a.m.–3 a.m. Majestic Star phone is (219)977-7777. Trump Casino is (219)977-8980.

HAMMOND

Adjoining Chicago's city limits on the east, Hammond has been an industrial adjunct to the great city since its inception. It was named for George Hammond, who operated a local slaughterhouse and devised a method for shipping dressed beef in refrigerated railroad cars. Many other factories eventually located here to take advantage of the city's excellent rail connections and its position on Lake Michigan.

Empress Casino, at 825 Empress Drive, off I-90. 8 a.m.-4 a.m. (219)473-7000.

LAWRENCEBURG

During the steamboat era on the Ohio, Lawrenceburg was notorious as a bawdy river town and Gamblers Row was renowned as a vice district. Things calmed down a bit as the nineteenth century progressed and by 1819 Lawrenceburg's proudest attraction was a three-story skyscraper, the tallest building in Indiana. The town later became a major center for whisky distilleries. Lawrenceburg has an especially well preserved historic district along the riverfront.

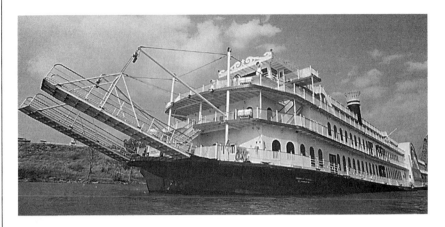

THE ARGOSY CASINO SITS AT ITS DOCK ON THE OHIO RIVER IN LAWRENCEBURG, INDIANA. (AP WIDE WORLD, TOM UHLMAN)

 Argosy Casino. Twenty-five miles west of downtown Cincinnati, Ohio, on U.S. 50. 9 a.m. to 1 a.m., Sunday to Thursday; open until 3 a.m., Friday and Saturday. (812)539-8000.

MICHIGAN CITY

The city grew up at the northern end of the Michigan Road, the pioneer trace through Indiana that connected the Ohio River ports to the Great Lakes. It lies on a Native American trail along the lakeshore dunes and was the site of a Potawatomi Village. Pioneers followed Trail Creek through the area, an extremely difficult overland passage to Chicago because of the sand and swampy terrain. It later became a resort area with a well-developed system of lakefront parks and recreational facilities. There are beaches, a zoo and historic lighthouse in Washington Park. Nearby is Lighthouse Place, an outlet mall with 120 stores.

 Blue Chip Casino, at the U.S. 12 bridge, on the lakefront. Thirty-five miles west of South Bend, by way of U.S. 20. Opening scheduled for August, 1997. Call for hours. (219)879-3402.

RISING SUN

A charming little town on Indiana's scenic River Road, Rising Sun got its name from the beauty of the morning light as it appeared over the hills of Kentucky across the water. The town faces due east, as does the nearby community of Aurora, whose early residents also named it after the dawn, but with a classical touch. This is one of the loveliest stretches of the river. A large number of residents of Swiss descent settled here to grow grapes for wine on its sunny slopes. The vineyards proved too costly to survive but many conoisseurs, including Henry Clay, were impressed by their quality.

Grand Victoria Casino and Hyatt Resort. 9 a.m.–1 a.m.
Forty miles southwest of Cincinnati, Ohio, by way of U.S. 50 and Indiana 56. (812)438-1234.

Michigan

There are a number of Native American casinos in Michigan. The city of Detroit is currently considering various proposals to build casinos in the Greektown area. For lottery information, contact the Michigan State Lottery.

 Michigan State Lottery, 101 E. Hillsdale, Lansing 48909, (517)335-5600. Sales: $1.4 billion. Proceeds: $549 million. 100% education.

BARAGA

The Ojibwa, or Chippewa as they are known in many areas, are the most numerous Native American group in North America, with a larger population now than they had at their first impact with Europeans. The meeting with the French, however, did touch off a migration of epic proportions. It sent the Ojibwa from their lands along Lake Huron on a westward course that led them through Michigan, Wisconsin and Minnesota. They drove the Sioux ahead of them, with results that left a deep imprint on the course of American history. This reservation, the largest in Michigan, lies at the head of scenic L'Anse Bay.

 Ojibwa Casino, (*Keweenaw Bay Indian Community*). Seventy miles west of Marquette along U.S. 41. (906)353-6333, (800) 323-8045.

BRIMLEY

This is another of the Chippewa communities on the Lake Superior shore.

Scenic Baraga

Outdoor activities abound in Baraga—camping, fishing, swimming, hiking, snowmobiling and skiing. For more information, contact the Baraga County Tourist and Recreation Association, 775 East Broad Street, L'Anse, (906)524-7444, or the following state parks.

- Baraga State Park, (906)353-6558
- The Copper Country State Forest, (906)353-6651
- Porcupine Mountain Wilderness State Park, (906)885-5275

 Bay Mills Resort and Casino, *(Bay Mills Indian Community).* Lake Shore Drive, twenty miles west of Sault Ste. Marie by way of Michigan 28 and 221. (906)248-3715.

CHRISTMAS

 Christmas Kewadin Casino,*(Sault Ste. Marie Tribe of Chippewa.)* 102 Candy Cane Lane, thirty-five miles east of Marquette on Michigan 28. (906)387-5475.

A branch of the tremendously popular Kewadin casino operation in Sault Ste. Marie.

HARRIS

This small Potawatomi community represents a remnant of the tribe that once dominated the southeastern shore of Lake Michigan and northern Indiana.

 Chip-In Casino, *(Hannahville Indian Community).* W399 Highway 2, 41. Fifteen miles west of Escanaba. (906)466-2941.

HAZEL PARK

 Hazel Park Harness Raceway. East from the 9 Mile Road exit of I-75, then north on Dequindre Road; eleven miles north of downtown Detroit. April–October. (248)398-1000.

ARCHITECT PAUL STEELMAN OF LAS VEGAS DISCUSSES THE PROPOSED PLANS FOR CASINOS IN DETROIT WITH THE DETROIT CASINO ADVISORY COMMITTEE. (AP WIDE WORLD, LINDA RADIN)

JACKSON

Jackson Harness Raceway. At the Fairgrounds, south from the Cooper Street exit of I-94; north of downtown. April–June, August–October. (517)788-4500.

LIVONIA

Ladbroke Detroit Race Course, thoroughbred track. South from I-96 at Middlebelt Road, seventeen miles west of downtown Detroit. March–November. (313)525-7300.

THE SOARING EAGLE CASINO IN MT. PLEASANT, MICHIGAN, ATTRACTS OVER 7,000 VISITORS A DAY. (AP WIDE WORLD, DAKE ATKINS)

MANISTIQUE

A Lake Michigan shore outpost of the Kewadin gambling empire.

 Manistique Kewadin. Fifty-five miles east of Escanaba on U.S. 2. (906)341-5510.

MT. PLEASANT

Mt. Pleasant Meadows, thoroughbred track. Off U.S. 27; sixty-three miles north of Lansing. Daily, May–September. (517)723-0012.

Soaring Eagle Casino, *(Saginaw Chippewa Tribe).* 6800 E. Soaring Eagle Boulevard, at the eastern edge of this community, fifty-three miles northwest of Saginaw, by way of Michigan 46 and U.S. 27. (517)775-4049.

At its opening in late 1996, Soaring Eagle was the largest casino in Michigan. The closest tribal operation to the huge population centers of the Lower Peninsula, it added a hotel complex

and convention center in 1997. This small band is the southern-most group of Chippewa in the state.

NORTHVILLE

 Northville Downs, harness racing. West from the 7 Mile Road exit of I-275; thirty miles northwest of downtown Detroit. January–April. (810)349-1000.

ST. IGNACE

Strategically placed, Kewadin Shores Casino catches the traffic entering the Upper Peninsula.

 Kewadin Shores Casino 3039 Mackinac Trail, just off the St. Ignace exit ramp of the Mackinac Bridge. (906)643-7071.

National Cherry Festival

In the 1890s, B.J. Morgan, a local farmer, began experimenting with growing tart red cherries. The moderating influence of Grand Traverse Bay on the local climate had been understood since the earliest French settlements. There is evidence of apple plantings here in the eighteenth century. Morgan suspected that cherries would thrive under the growing conditions.

He was right. By the turn of the century, Traverse City was the top cherry-producing area in the country. It was certainly the most intensively planted—by necessity. Just a few miles inland, the harsh northern winters would not support the crop. Much of the old Mission Peninsula, the slender finger of land that divides the bay into two branches, was turned into orchards as was the narrow band of farmland on the eastern and western margins of the bay. In recent years the biggest threat to the cherry orchards has been tourism rather than the weather. Traverse City is now a major resort area and much farmland has been lost to condominiums and golf courses. But the town still celebrates the fruit during the first full week in July with three parades, band competitions, entertainment in the city's waterfront parks, a pageant and coronation of the Cherry Queen, cherry pit spitting contest and cherries served in a variety of ways.

Traverse City is located about fifty miles west of I-75, by way of Michigan 72. For more festival information, contact The National Cherry Festival, 108 West Grandview Parkway, Traverse City 49684, (616)947-4230. (From *Historic Festivals: A Traveler's Guide*, by George Cantor, Visible Ink Press, 1996.)

SAULT STE. MARIE

The biggest gambling operation in the Upper Peninsula, with branches all across the north and a customer base that reaches into Canada.

 Vegas Kewadin Casino. 2186 Shunk Road. East of I-75. (906)632-0530.

SUTTONS BAY

A great trading nation, the Ottawa were the most populous Native group in Michigan's northern Lower Peninsula in the eighteenth century. Pontiac, who led the great rebellion against Britain in 1763, was a member of this tribe. Many Ottawa still reside along the Lake Michigan shore in the Grand and Little Traverse Bay areas.

 Leelenau Sands Casino, *(Grand Traverse Tribal Nation).* 2521 N. West Bayshore Drive, on Michigan 22, twenty miles north of Traverse City. (616)271-4104.

SWARTZ CREEK

 Sports Creek Raceway, harness racing. Off I-69; eight miles southwest of downtown Flint. January–April, October–December. (810)635-3333.

TRAVERSE CITY

Opened in the summer of 1997, this casino is run by the same group that operates the Sutton's Bay casino.

 Turtle Creek Casino, *(Grand Traverse Tribal Nation).* On Michigan 72; fifteen miles east of Traverse City. Daily, 8 a.m.–2:30 a.m. (800)893-2946.

WATERSMEET

 Lac Vieux Desert Casino, *(Lac Vieux Desert Band of Lake Superior Chippewa).* A small operation close to the Wisconsin border. Chote Road, fifty-five miles east of Ironwood, on U.S. 2. (906)358-4226.

Minnesota

Native American casinos are located through–out Minnesota. State lottery information can be obtained by contacting the Minnesota State Lottery.

 Minnesota State Lottery, 2645 Long Lake Road, Roseville 55113, (612)635-8100. Sales: $376 million. Proceeds: $89 million. 70% General Fund. 30% Environmental and Natural Resources Fund.

CARLTON

The Fond du Lac Chippewa Reservation lies along the St. Louis River, a few miles inland from the western end of Lake Superior.

 Black Bear Casino, *(Fond du Lac reservation).* 601 Highway 210. Twenty miles southwest of Duluth on I-35 and Minnesota 210. (218)878-2412.

CASS LAKE

The Leech Lake reservation operates three casinos, two at the administrative center in Cass Lake and a third at the southern end of the sprawling northern Minnesota reserve, in Walker.

 Che–We Casino and Palace Casino, *(Leech Lake Band of Chippewa).* Fifteen miles east of Bemidji on U.S. 2. (218)335-8338, 335-6787.

DULUTH

An urban casino operated by the reservation that lies on the out-skirts of the city.

Ni-Min-Win Ojibwa Festival

More Native Americans claim affiliation with the Ojibwa, or Chippewa, than any other tribal group. An estimated 160,000 persons in the northern United States and Canada identify themselves with the tribe.

There are seven Ojibwa reservations in Minnesota. The largest of them, the Leech Lake and White Earth Reservations, take in big chunks of prime inland lake country. Both bands have built thriving tourist business, and also engage in wild rice cultivation and other enterprises. On the third weekend of August the various bands assemble in Duluth, near the Fond du Lac Reservation, for one of the biggest tribal gatherings in the Midwest. The Ni-Min-Win Ojibwa Festival features traditional dancing and is also a good opportunity to shop for Ojibwa crafts and artwork, especially black ash baskets. The Ni-Min-Win celebration is held in various locations around Duluth, usually along the Lake Superior shore. Call (800)438-5884 or (218)722-4011.

 Fond du Luth Casino, *(Fond Du Lac Chippewa).* 129 E. Superior Street, downtown Duluth. (218)722-0280.

GRAND PORTAGE

The Chippewa have long operated a tourist lodge in this semi-wilderness on Lake Superior at the edge of the Boundary Waters Area. Grand Portage was the earliest settlement in Minnesota, a trade center for Native Americans and French voyageurs. It was the depot where goods were transferred from the smaller inland canoes to the larger Great Lakes craft.

 Grand Portage Casino, *(Grand Portage Band of Chippewa).* 150 miles northeast of Duluth, in the Arrowhead of Minnesota, on the Ontario border. (218)475-2441.

GRANITE FALLS

The Upper Sioux Reservation preserves a remnant of the Santee, or Eastern branch of the Sioux family. French explorers found the Sioux around the Mille Lacs area of central Minnesota. Ongoing wars with the Ojibwa drove them steadily west and south. The Santee bands, especially the Sisseton and Wahpeton, settled along the Minnesota River. When clashes with white settlers broke out at the Lower Sioux Agency in the 1860s, the Upper Sioux tried to remain neutral. The aftermath of the war was so bitter that most of them were removed to land in the Dakotas. Only a small portion remains here.

 Firefly Creek Casino, *(Upper Sioux Community)*. One-hundred thirty miles west of Minneapolis, by way of Minnesota 7 and 23. (320)564-2121.

HINCKLEY

An Interstate-friendly branch of the Mille Lacs gambling operation, centered on the main reservation to the west.

 Grand Casino Hinckley, *(Mille Lacs Band of Chippewa)*. 777 Lady Luck Drive. Eighty miles north of St. Paul, by way of I-35 and County Road 3. (612)384-7771.

MAHNOMEN

White Earth has the greatest land area of the Chippewa reserves in Minnesota.

 Shooting Star Casino, *(White Earth Band of Chippewa)*. Eighty miles northeast of Fargo, North Dakota by way of U.S. 75 and Minnesota 200. (218)935-2701.

MORTON

This was the point of origin for the infamous Sioux uprising of 1862, which resulted in the murder of several white settlers, the hanging of thirty-eight Sioux and the removal of all the tribe's Santee branch to the Dakotas. The Lower Agency was composed of the Wakpekute and Mdewakanton divisions. A few of them managed to trickle back to Minnesota after the deprivation and disease suffered on the Plains and they were granted a small tract of land here.

 Jackpot Junction, *(Lower Sioux Indian Community)*. 110 miles southwest of Minneapolis, by way of U.S. 212, Minnesota 5 and 19. (507)644-7761.

THE ENTRANCE TO THE GRAND CASINO MILLE LACS. (COURTESY OF THE GRAND CASINO MILLE LACS)

ONAMIA

Mille Lacs was the site of the decisive battle between the Sioux and Chippewa invaders, somewhere around 1750. It established the Chippewa as the dominant tribe in Minnesota and pushed their rivals west onto the Great Plains. A small Chippewa reserve was established on the west side of the lake.

 Grand Casino Mille Lacs, 777 Grand Avenue. Ninety-five miles north of Minneapolis, on U.S. 169. (800)626-5825.

PRIOR LAKE

Just beyond the suburbs of the Twin Cities, this small community is a remnant of the Santee Sioux.

 Little 6 Bingo, *(Shakopee Mdewakanton Sioux Community)*. 2400 Mystic Lake Boulevard, thirty miles southwest of Minneapolis, by way of I-35 and Minnesota 13. (612)445-9000.

RED LAKE

This is the largest of the Red Lake Reservation tracts, which are scattered through northwestern Minnesota.

 Red Lake Casino, *(Red Lake Band of Chippewas).* Thirty-five miles north of Bemidji, on Minnesota 89. (218)679-2500.

RED WING

This is a Mdewakanton Sioux operation, in recreational boating country along the Mississippi River.

 Treasure Island Casino, *(Prairie Island Indian Community).* 5734 Sturgeon Lake Road, fifty miles southeast of St. Paul, on U.S. 61. (612)385-6300.

THIEF RIVER FALLS

 River Road Casino, *(Red Lake Band of Chippewa).* Located a few miles west of the main Red Lake Reservation tract. Rural Road 3, seventy miles northeast of Grand Forks, North Dakota by way of Minnesota 32 and U.S. 2. (218)681-4062.

TOWER

 Fortune Bay Casino, *(Bois Forte Band of Chippewa).* Located in the iron range, near Vermilion Lake. 1430 Bois Forte Road, fifty miles northeast of Hibbing, by way of U.S. 169 and Minnesota 1. (218)753-6400.

WALKER

 Northern Lights Casino, *(Leech Lake Band of Chippewa).* Forty miles south of Bemidji, by way of U.S. 2 and Minnesota 371. This is the southernmost of the three casinos sited on the Leech Lake reservation. (218)547-2744.

WARROAD

The northernmost point in the forty-eight contiguous states is the Northwest Angle, which is part of the Red Lake Reservation, on the far side of Lake of the Woods. The casino is located along the lakeshore.

 Lake of the Woods Casino, *(Red Lake Band of Chippewa.)* 1001 1/2 Lake Street, 106 miles west of International Falls, on Minnesota 11. (218)386-3381.

Ohio

Gambling in Ohio is limited to placing bets at the track or purchasing lottery tickets. Contact the Ohio State Lottery for ticket information.

 Ohio State Lottery, 615 W. Superior Avenue, Cleveland 44113, (216)787-3200. Sales: $2.3 billion. Proceeds: $727 million. 100% education.

CINCINNATI

 River Downs, thoroughbred track. At 6301 Kellogg Road (U.S. 52), east from the Columbia Parkway and downtown Cincinnati. April–November. (513)232-8000.

COLUMBUS

 Scioto Downs, harness racing. At 6000 S. High Street (U.S. 23), just south of I-270; south of downtown Columbus. May–September. (614)491-2515.

GROVE CITY

 Beulah Park, thoroughbred track. Off Harrisburg Pike (U.S. 62); nine miles southwest of downtown Columbus. January–May. (614)871-9600.

LEBANON

Lebanon Raceway, harness racing. At 665 N. Broadway, off I-71 at the Lebanon exit; thirty miles northeast of downtown Cincinnati. January–May and September–October. (513)932-4936.

NORTH RANDALL

Thistledown Racing Club, thoroughbred track. At 21501 Emery Road, off I-271 and north of I-480, southeast of downtown Cleveland. March–December. (216)662-8600.

NORTHFIELD

Northfield Park, harness racing. On Northfield Road, off the Northfield exit of I-271; fifteen miles southeast of downtown Cleveland. All year. (216)467-4101.

TOLEDO

Raceway Park, harness racing. At 5700 Telegraph Road (U.S. 24); west from the Alexis Road exit from I-75; north of downtown Toledo. March–December. (419)476-7751.

West Virginia

The state has licensed casino operations at one horse track and two dog tracks. The only machines permitted are video poker and Keno. For state lottery information, contact the West Virginia State Lottery.

 West Virginia State Lottery, 312 MacCorkle Avenue SE, Charleston 25327, (304)558-0500. Sales: $210 million. Proceeds: $61 million. 69% education; 16.2% tourism; 14.8% senior citizens.

CHARLES TOWN

Except during the Civil War, there has been horse racing in Charles Town since 1786, making this track's lineage one of the oldest in North America. Open all year.

 Charles Town Races, thoroughbred track. On U.S. 340, east of town; twenty-seven miles southwest of Frederick, Maryland. (304) 725-7001.

CHARLESTON

 Tri-State Greyhound Track. Twelve miles west on I-64. The racetrack seats 4,000. (304) 725-7001.

CHESTER

This is a pottery town established in 1896 and given its name simply because it is easy to remember.

Mountaineer Race Track and Resort, thoroughbred track. Across the Ohio River from East Liverpool, Ohio, then south seven miles on West Virginia 2. The Mountaineer has an adjoining motel. Open all year. (304) 387-2400.

WHEELING

The island was part of the original Wheeling settlement by the Zane Brothers in 1769. They called it "a vision of paradise." Those who suffered through its three major floods called it something else. After the inundation of 1936, flood control measures were put in. Wheeling Downs opened a year later on the grounds of the former State Fair Park.

Wheeling Downs. The greyhound track is at the southern end of Wheeling Island, which is in the midst of the Ohio River, and is reached by eastbound I-70 from the city. (304) 232-2050.

Wisconsin

Native American reservations offer casino gambling in Wisconsin. To purchase lottery tickets, contact the Wisconsin State Lottery.

 Wisconsin State Lottery, 1802 W. Beltline Highway, Madison 53708, (608)266-7777. Sales: $482 million. Proceeds: $156 million. 100% property tax relief.

BARABOO

Ho-Chunk is a name by which the Winnebago people refer to themselves, a term that is sometimes translated as "people of the real speech." They are distant relatives of the Sioux and also related culturally to the Sac & Fox. Living around the Green Bay area when the Europeans arrived, the tribe was gradually driven west and eventually placed on a reservation in Nebraska. But many of the Winnebago drifted back to Wisconsin over the years and in the 1930s, the federal government purchased several homesites for them in localities around the state. They operate three casinos in Wisconsin.

 Hochunk Casino, *(Ho-Chunk Nation).* South 3214A Highway 12, fifteen miles south of Wisconsin Dells on U.S. 12. (608)356-6210.

BAYFIELD

Overlooking the Apostle Islands National Lakeshore, the Red Cliff Reservation is an especially scenic part of Lake Superior resort country. There is also an arts and cultural center in the town of Red Cliff.

 Isle Vista Casino, *(Red Cliff Band of Lake Superior Chippewa).* Eighty miles east of Superior, on Wisconsin 13. (715)779-3712.

Circus World Museum

The circus came to town in 1882 and never left. That's the year that five local boys, the Ringling Brothers, organized their first traveling show. They advertised it as "moral, elevating, instructive and fascinating." It was certainly all that and more. It played to fifty-nine people on its first night. The Ringlings had show business in their blood. They put their show on wheels and spent the summer touring the upper Midwest. Within six years they were able to afford thirty railroad cars, a wild animal show and a big tent.

The arrival of the circus in these rural communities, long before the age of cheap transportation and mass communications, was an event of such magnitude that the entire calendar seemed to be shaped around it. The parade, the band, the clowns, the midway. The Ringlings were masters at building up a sense of anticipation by sending in advance men to crank up the locals. By the turn of the century, they had, in effect, divided the country with their chief rival, Barnum and Bailey. The Ringlings took the western half. Then in 1907, Bailey's widow sold her share of Barnum and Bailey to the Ringlings and the two shows combined to form "The Greatest Show on Earth."

Baraboo remained the winter home of the circus for eleven more years until the Ringlings became involved in Florida real estate and transferred their headquarters to Sarasota. Many of the former circus warehouses were converted to other uses. Other original buildings form the core of Circus World, a look at the historical development of the shows. And in summer, the excitement of an old-time traveling circus is magically recreated at the place where this slice of Americana was born.

Baraboo is about fifty miles northwest of Madison, by way of U.S. 12. Circus World is located at 426 Water Street. Circus performances are given daily, May through September 7th, 9–6; with shows extending until 10 p.m. mid-July to mid-August. The mueum exhibits are open year-round. Admission is $11.95 for adults, $10.95 for seniors, $5.95 for children ages 3–12, and children under the age of three are free. For more information, call (608)356-0800. (From *Pop Culture Landmarks: A Traveler's Guide*, by George Cantor, Visible Ink Press, 1995)

BLACK RIVER FALLS

 Majestic Pines Casino, *(Ho-Chunk Nation).* Highway 54 East, off I-94, fifty-five miles southeast of Eau Claire. (715)284-2721. Located near another of the Ho-Chunk townsites.

BOWLER

The reservation is inhabited by descendants of two East Coast tribes, who were among the first to make contact with Europeans. The Stockbridge were known as Mahicans and were given this name from the western Massachusetts near which they lived. The Munsee were a division of the Delaware nation, which once was the most populous group in the Middle Atlantic colonies. After being driven steadily west for two centuries, the two groups combined to purchase this reservation land from the Menominee in 1832 to obtain secure title.

 Mohican North Star Casino, *(Stockbridge-Munsee Community).* W. 12180 County Road A, forty miles east of Wausau, by way of Wisconsin 28 and county roads. (715)793-4090.

DANBURY

The small community is situated on the St. Croix Scenic Riverway, on the Minnesota border.

 Hole in the Wall Casino, *(St. Croix Chippewa Indians of Wisconsin).* Sixty miles south of Superior, on Wisconsin 35. (715)656-3444.

HAYWARD

The Chippewa settlement is situated in splendid lake and forest country in northwestern Wisconsin, amid some of the finest sport fishing areas in the Midwest.

 Lac Courte Oreilles Casino, *(Lac Courte Oreille Band of Lake Superior Chippewa).* Seventy miles southeast of Superior, by way of U.S. 53 and Wisconsin 77. (715)634-5643.

KESHENA

The Menominee, related by language to the Chippewa, managed to chart a middle course between trading with the Europeans and avoiding the ruinous inter-tribal wars that depleted many of their neighbors. While other tribes were forced west, the Menominee managed to secure reservation lands in 1854. While much of that tract was taken from them and given to Eastern tribes, the Menominee still have built up a lumbering industry here.

 Menominee Nation Casino. Forty-five miles northwest of Green Bay, by way of Wisconsin 29 and 47. (715)799-3600.

LAC DU FLAMBEAU

Magnificent lake country surrounded by national forest amid a prime fishing area.

 Lake of the Torches Casino, *(Lac De Flambeau Band of Lake Superior Chippewa).* Forty-five miles south of Ironwood, Michigan, by way of U.S. 51 and Wisconsin 47. (715)588-3303.

MILWAUKEE

Several Potawatomi bands are scattered around their historic homelands, south of Green Bay. The vast majority of the tribe now live in Oklahoma and Kansas.

 Potawatomi Bingo & Casino, 1721 W. Canal Street, in central Milwaukee. (414)645-6888.

NEKOOSA

 Rainbow Casino, *(Ho-Chunk Nation).* One of three Winnebago casinos run by the scattered townsites in the state. 949 County Road G., twenty-one miles west of U.S. 51, by way of Wisconsin 73. (715)886-4560.

ODANAH

The Bad River Reservation, on scenic land bordered by Lake Superior and Chequamgon Bay, is the largest of the Chippewa tracts in the state.

Buffalo Arts Center

The Buffalo Arts Center is an exceptionally well-designed museum facility that concentrates on contemporary arts and crafts of this Chippewa group. The reservation occupies a very scenic portion of the Bayfield Peninsula. From the town of Red Cliff there are fine views across Chequamegon Bay to the Apostle Islands National Lakeshore.

Red Cliff is on Wisconsin 13, about three miles north of the resort town of Bayfield, starting point of boat trips to the Apostle Islands. The museum is open daily from 10–4, May through September. Admission is $3.00. Call (715)779-5805 for more information. (From *North American Indian Landmarks: A Traveler's Guide*, by George Cantor, Visible Ink Press, 1993)

 Bad River Casino, *(Bad River Band of Lake Superior Chippewa).* Thirty miles west of Ironwood, Michigan, on U.S. 2. (715)682-7111.

ONEIDA

The Oneida are a branch of the Iroquois Confederacy, originally based in the area between Syracuse and Utica, in New York. Alone among the confederacy, they supported the American cause. Nonetheless, concerned by the onrush of settlement, most of the tribe moved to Wisconsin in the 1820s and bought land from the Menominee. Much of it was subsequently lost but large groups of Oneida still live in the Green Bay area.

 Oneida Bingo, *(Oneida Tribe).* On the western outskirts of Green Bay, on Wisconsin 54. (414)490-3505.

TURTLE LAKE

 St. Croix Casino, *(St. Croix Chippewa Indians).* One of two casinos operated by the St. Croix band in the northwestern part of Wisconsin. 777 Highway 8, seventy miles northwest of Eau Claire, by way of U.S. 53 and 8. (715)986-4777.

WABENO

This small Powataomi community is located in the heart of the Nicolet National Forest.

 Northern Lights Casino, *(Forest County Potawatomi Community).* Highway 32, ninety miles northwest of Green Bay, by way of U.S. 141, Wisconsin 64 and 32. (800)487-9522.

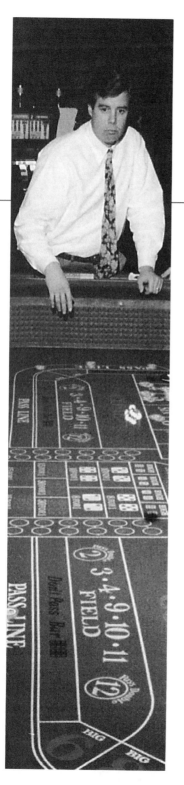

GREAT PLAINS

Iowa
Kansas
Missouri
Nebraska
North Dakota
Oklahoma
South Dakota
Texas

Iowa

1. Prairie Meadows Casino, Altoona
2. Lady Luck Casino, Bettendorf
3. Mississippi Belle II, Clinton
4. Ameristar II, Council Bluffs
5. Harvey's Casino, Council Bluffs
6. Bluffs Run Casino, Council Bluffs
7. The President Riverboat Casino, Davenport
8. The Bix Biederbecke Festival, Davenport
9. Diamond Jo Casino, Dubuque
10. Catfish Bend Casino, Fort Madison-Burlington
11. Miss Marquette Riverboat Casino, Marquette
12. Casino Omaha, Onawa
13. Belle of Sioux City Casino, Sioux City
14. Winna Vegas Casino, Sloan
15. Meskwaki Casino, Tama

Kansas

16. Eureka Downs, Eureka
17. Golden Eagle Casino, Horton
18. Woodlands, Kansas City
19. Prairie Band Potawatomi Casino and Bingo, Mayetta
20. Iowa Tribe Games, White Cloud

Missouri

23. Casino Aztar, Caruthersville
25. Argosy Casino, Kansas City
26. Flamingo Casino, Kansas City
27. Harrah's North Kansas City Casino, Kansas City
28. Sam's Town Casino, Kansas City
29. Station Casino, Kansas City
31. Harrah's Casino St. Louis, Maryland Heights
32. Players Casino, Maryland Heights
33. Station Casino, St. Charles
34. St. Jo Frontier Casino, St. Joseph
35. President Casino on the Admiral, St. Louis
36. Border Town Casino, Seneca

North Dakota

37. Wild Rose Casino, Belmont
38. Prairie Knights Casino, Fort Yates
39. Dakota Magic Casino, Hankinson
40. International Inn, Minot
41. Four Bears Casino, New Town
42. Spirit Lake Casino, Spirit Lake

Nebraska

43. Fonner Park, Grand Island
44. Ak-Sar-Ben Horse Track, Omaha (closed)
45. Rosebud Casino, Valentine

Oklahoma

46. Na-I-Sha Games, Anadarko
47. Bingo Outposts, Catoosa, Roland, Siloam Springs
48. Clinton High Stakes Bingo, Clinton
49. Lucky Star Bingo, Concho
50. Watonga Bingo, Watonga
51. The Gaming Center, Ada
52. The Goldsby Gaming Center, Norman
53. Sulphur Gaming Center and Chickasaw Motor Inn, Sulphur
54. Touso Ishto Gaming, Thackerville
55. Choctaw Bingo-Arrowhead, Canada
56. Choctaw Bingo Palace, Durant
57. Choctaw Bingo, Idabel
58. Choctaw Bingo, Pocola
59. Comanche Nation Games, Lawton
60. Bristow Indian Bingo, Bristow
61. Checotah Bingo, Checotah
62. Eufaula Bingo, Eufaula
63. Muskogee Bingo, Muskogee
64. Okmulgee Bingo, Okmulgee
65. Tulsa Bingo, Tulsa
66. Cimarron Bingo, Perkins
67. Kaw Bingo Enterprise, Kaw City
68. Kiowa Bingo, Carnegie
69. Ponca Tribal Bingo, Ponca City
70. Firelake Entertainment City, Shawnee
71. Foxfire Inc., Edmond
72. Seminole Bingo, Seminole
73. Seneca-Cayuga Gaming Operation, Miami
74. Thunderbird Entertainment Center, Norman
75. Loyal Shawnee Bingo, Vinita
76. Remington Park, Oklahoma City
77. Fair Meadows, Tulsa

South Dakota

78. Dakota Connection, Agency Village
79. The Bullock, Deadwood
80. The Dakota Territory, Deadwood

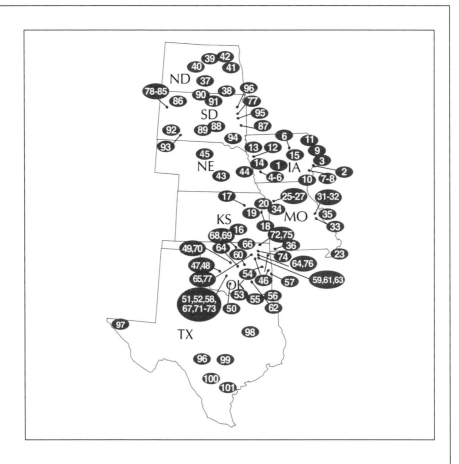

81. The Franklin Hotel and Gambling
    Hall, Deadwood
82. Gold Dust, Deadwood
83. Golddigger's Hotel and Gambling,
    Deadwood
84. Midnight Star, Deadwood
85. The Mineral Palace, Deadwood
86. Wild Bill's Bar, Deadwood
87. C.R.S.T. Bingo, Eagle Butte
88. Royal River Casino, Flandreau
89. Lode Star Casino, Fort Thompson
90. Golden Buffalo Casino, Lower Brule
91. Bear Soldier Bingo, McLaughlin

92. Grand River Casino, Mobridge
93. Prairie Wind Casino, Oelrichs
94. Children's Village Bingo, Pine Ridge
95. Fort Randall Casino, Wagner
96. Dakota Sioux Casino, Watertown

Texas

97. Bandera Downs, Bandera (closed)
98. Speaking Rock Casino, El Paso
99. Sam Houston Race Park, Houston
100. Manor Downs, Manor
101. Retama Park, San Antonio

Iowa

Under terms of Iowa's gaming laws, not only riverboats but three land-based casinos and horse and dog pari-mutuel tracks are legal. All forms of slot machines, blackjack, craps, roulette and poker are permissible. Most casinos are open for twenty-four hours. Some riverboats are seasonal and actually leave the dock for two-hour cruises during the summer months. Contact the Iowa State Lottery for lottery information.

 Iowa State Lottery, 2015 Grand Avenue, Des Moines 50312, (317)281-7900. Sales: $190 million. Proceeds: $51 million. 100% General fund.

ALTOONA

 Prairie Meadows Casino and thoroughbred track. Nine miles east of downtown Des Moines, at I-80, exit 142. Daily, open twenty-four hours. This casino owns Iowa's only license to operate on the grounds of a pari-mutuel horse racing track. The track is open daily, May–August. The complex is located in the northeastern suburbs of Des Moines.(515) 967-1000.

BETTENDORF

When the Bettendorf Axle and Wagon Co. decided to locate here in 1903, its influence on the community was so profound that the place decided to change it name. The quiet town of Gilbert became Bettendorf, and it continues to thrive under that name as one of the Quad Cities along the Mississippi River. Buffalo Bill's boyhood home is just north of town, along the Great River Road, U.S. 67.

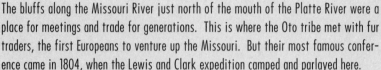

Council Monument

The bluffs along the Missouri River just north of the mouth of the Platte River were a place for meetings and trade for generations. This is where the Oto tribe met with fur traders, the first Europeans to venture up the Missouri. But their most famous conference came in 1804, when the Lewis and Clark expedition camped and parlayed here.

The place that the Oto chiefs met with Lewis and Clark was known as Hart's Bluff. The name Council Bluffs had been given to the whole line of hills on the east bank of the river, and in 1852, the newly formed town on this site chose that name for itself. The monument depicting the historic conference between Lewis and Clark and the Oto chiefs is north of the city center, along the bluffs, on Rainbow Drive. It is easily accessible from Eighth Street. (From *North American Indian Landmarks,* by George Cantor, Visible Ink Press, 1993)

 Lady Luck Casino. Off I-74, at the State Street landing. Daily, open twenty-four hours. Boarding every two hours, starting at 8:30 a.m., May–October. (319)358-7280.

CLINTON

Clinton grew up as a lumbering port where logs that floated down the Mississippi from the forests of Minnesota and Wisconsin were milled. It was a major stop for riverboats, too. Early settlers called it New York, but upon reflection renamed it, instead, for a governor of New York, DeWitt Clinton. The city celebrates its heritage with Riverboat Days on the nearest weekend to the Fourth of July.

 Mississippi Belle II. Off U.S. 67 at the 6th Avenue North exit. Monday to Thursday, 9 a.m.–2 a.m.; open Friday and Saturday until 4 a.m. Two-hour cruises daily at 1 p.m., mid-May to mid-October. (319)243-9000.

COUNCIL BLUFFS

Lewis and Clark met with local Native American leaders on the heights above the Missouri River during their expedition of 1804. For decades afterwards, the bluffs became a traditional place for such parleys and thus were given their present name. This was also the location of a large Mormon community in the 1840s, but it packed up in 1852 to join the main religious contingent in Utah. Council Bluffs was chosen as the eastern terminus of the first intercontinental railroad and during the Civil War years westward-bound commerce flowed through the town.

Ameristar II, at 2200 River Road, from exit 52 on I-29. Daily, twenty-four hours. (712)322-9984.

Bluffs Run Casino and greyhound track, off I-29 at the 24th Street Exit. Daily, twenty-four hours. (800)238-2946.

Harvey's Casino, at exit 53A of I-29, just south of the I-480 bridge to Omaha, Nebraska. Daily, twenty-four hours. (712)329-6000.

DAVENPORT

Largest of the Quad Cities, Davenport opened for settlement after the Black Hawk War. The Sac & Fox tribes were forced to cede most of their holdings along the west bank of the Mississippi and Col. George Davenport, an Army officer who had been stationed at Rock Island, bought the tract that became this city. When jazz came up the river on the boats from New Orleans, this was one of its more significant stops. Davenport-born Bix Beiderbecke absorbed what he heard and became one of the most influential and widely-copied horn players of the 1920s, and the fictional model for music-obsessed young men who died too young. Davenport recalls his legacy with a riverfront jazz festival on the last weekend of July. There are also a number of scale model riverboat reproductions in the Putnam Museum of History, at 1717 W. 12th Street.

The President Riverboat Casino, at River Drive and Brady Street. Monday to Friday, 8 a.m.–2 a.m.; weekends, twenty-four hours. Cruises daily at 8:30 a.m., May–October. This boat also features Keno and a separate poker parlor, within an unusually spacious 27,000 square foot casino area. (319)322-BOAT.

DUBUQUE

The oldest European settlement in Iowa, Dubuque started off as a lead mine in 1788 under a concession from the King of Spain to Julien Dubuque. The Sac & Fox barred any further occupancy, but after their defeat in the Black Hawk War of 1832, the settlers and miners rolled in. Dubuque's economy was always tied to the river. It is the home of the Mississippi River Museum, one of the best of its kind. Located in the Ice Har-

THE DIAMOND JO CASINO WAITS FOR THE NEXT CRUISE. (COURTESY OF THE DIAMOND JO CASINO)

bor area, adjacent to the casino, the museum contains historic riverboats, a boatyard and the National Rivers Hall of Fame, saluting individuals whose accomplishments are linked to America's rivers. The city is backed by high bluffs which open out on fine views over Illinois and Wisconsin.

Diamond Jo Casino. North of U.S. 20 at the U.S. 151 and 61 exit, then follow signs to Ice Harbor. Sunday to Tuesday, 9 a.m.–2 a.m.; Wednesday and Thursday, open until 4 a.m.; Friday and Saturday, open twenty-four hours. Two-hour cruises begin at 10 a.m., Monday to Friday, May–October. (319)583-7005.

FORT MADISON-BURLINGTON

During the more popular summer months, the riverboat docks in Fort Madison. This is a history-filled river town, which started out as a U.S. Army outpost in 1808. It was burned to the ground five years later during an Indian attack. Later on it became an important logging port and a point of trans-shipment for beef headed east on the Santa Fe Railroad. The town has an extensive historic district with several late Victorian buildings. The Historic Center in the former Santa Fe terminal has several exhibits relating to life on the river.

Burlington's site became the location of a fur-trading post the same year Fort Madison opened. It thrived because of excellent river and rail connections, becoming the capital and later a center of commerce for the Iowa Territory. As a result, Burlington has as fine a collection of Victorian neighborhoods as any city on the Mississippi. Among the most picturesque is Snake Alley, a road that winds down from the bluffs to the riverfront through a series of loops. It is the

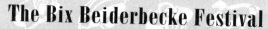

The Bix Beiderbecke Festival

He was the prototype of the doomed jazz artist, a brilliant musician with a self-destructive drive that ran deeper than the Mississippi. Leon Bix Beiderbecke grew up in Davenport and heard the music. Just as the old cliche said, it was coming up the river from New Orleans. He learned to play it on the showboats that still wheeled along the river in the 1920s.

In those years, jazz was music played predominantly by black musicians. Formally trained whites seemed to lack the improvisational ability that lay at the heart of jazz. But Bix Beiderbecke was brilliant with it. His cornet solos and unique phrasing, heard on scratchy old discs more than sixty years after their first recording, still have the power to charm. He inspired an entire generation of young composers and artists, among them Hoagy Carmichael and Benny Goodman.

His life, which was the model for the classic film *Young Man with a Horn,* was cut short at the age of twenty-eight. Filling the well of his talent with alcohol and riotous nights was more than his body could support. During the last full weekend in July, Davenport recalls its local jazzman with this musical tribute of concerts and riverboat races. Most of the events take place in LeClaire Park, along the riverfront. For more information, contact the Bix Biederbecke Memorial Society, P.O. Box 3688, Davenport 52808, (319)324-7170. (From *Historic Festivals: A Traveler's Guide,* by George Cantor, Visible Ink Press, 1996)

scene of an annual art fair and historic celebration on Memorial Day weekend.

 Catfish Bend Casino. The riverboat is berthed at Fort Madison Landing, on U.S. 61 at 6th Street, May–October for two-hour cruises. During the rest of the year it is stationary at Big Muddy's Landing, on North Front Street, Burlington. The two cities are located twenty miles apart, on U.S. 61. Wednesday to Sunday, open twenty-four hours; Monday and Tuesday, 8 a.m.–2 a.m. Two-hour cruise daily, at 10 a.m. when it is berthed at Fort Madison. (319)372-2946.

MARQUETTE

The little town is tucked into the bluffs of the Mississippi in an area that figured in both Native American and European history. The area was first inhabited by a mound-building people who shaped their work in the form of animals and birds. It is the most extensive such grouping in the Midwest. It was also at this point that the French explorers, Louis Joliet and Fr. Jacques Marquette, first entered Iowa in their voyage of 1673.

Miss Marquette Riverboat Casino, just south of the U.S. 18 bridge, sixty-eight miles north of Dubuque. Daily, twenty-four hours. (800)496-8238.

ONAWA

Although tribal lands are located in Nebraska, the Omaha have set up their casino in the more liberal gaming environment of Iowa. The tribe's name means "going against the current" and refers to an historic split among various migrating groups at the junction of the Ohio and Mississippi Rivers. Those who turned north along the Mississippi were called Omaha, and later split into Osage, Kansa, Ponca and Omaha tribes. They occupied the Platte and Niobrara valleys of Nebraska but were forced to cede their lands in 1854.

 Casino Omaha, *(Omaha Tribe).* 1 Blackbird Bend, thirty-eight miles south of Sioux City, on I-29. (712)423-3700.

SIOUX CITY

The market center for a three-state cattle-raising and grain-growing area, Sioux City sits at the confluence of the Missouri and Big Sioux Rivers. This was the burial place of the only casualty of the Lewis and Clark Expedition. Sgt. Charles Floyd died here in 1804 of a ruptured appendix and the obelisk that marks his place of rest is the oldest registered national historic landmark in the country. At the Sgt. Floyd Welcome Center, on I-29, dioramas explain the workings of the Missouri River. The city also celebrates a River-Cade Festival in the last week of July.

Belle of Sioux City Casino, exit I-29 at Larson Park Drive. Sunday to Thursday, 9:30 a.m.–4 a.m.; Friday and Saturday, open until 6 a.m. Daily cruises at 10 a.m. and noon, April–September. (712)255-0080.

SLOAN

The Winnebago originally lived in the area around Green Bay, Wisconsin but, eventually, was transported into Iowa and Nebraska.

They share reservation lands with the Omaha in Nebraska, and like their neighbors, set up a casino in Iowa.

 Winna Vegas Casino, *(Winnebago Tribe).* 1500-330 St., twenty miles south of Sioux City on I-29. (712)428-9466.

TAMA

The Sac & Fox migrated southwest from Wisconsin's Lake Superior shore, where they waged constant battles with the French and Ojibwa. Caught up in Black Hawk's War of the 1830s, they continued on into Iowa. But lead mines they operated successfully near Dubuque were seized and they were forced to remove themselves to Kansas. A small group returned to Iowa in 1859 and reservation lands were set aside for them.

 Meskwaki Casino, *(Sac & Fox Tribe).* 1504 305th Street, fifty miles west of Cedar Rapids on U.S. 30. (515)484-2108.

Kansas

Gaming is available at Native American casinos, in addition to betting on the horses at the track. For lottery information, contact the Kansas State Lottery.

 Kansas State Lottery, 128 N. Kansas Avenue, Topeka, 66603, (913) 296-5700. Sales: $182 million. Proceeds: $58 million. 86% economic development and corrections; 14% General fund.

EUREKA

 Eureka Downs, thoroughbred track. Off U.S. 54; sixty-two miles east of Wichita. May–July. (316)583-5528.

HORTON

Closely allied the Sac & Fox, the Kickapoo joined the other tribes in their resistance to the French and later the Americans in Black Hawk's War. Forced to move ever westward, they were scattered among reservation lands in Kansas, Oklahoma and Mexico.

 Golden Eagle Casino, *(Kickapoo Nation in Kansas).* Fifty-five miles north of Topeka, by way of U.S. 75. (913)486-2131.

KANSAS CITY

 Woodlands, thoroughbred track. Off I-435, at 99th Street and Leavenworth Road, fifteen miles southwest of downtown Kansas City. August–November. (913)299-9797.

HUNDREDS OF CUSTOMERS READY TO TRY THEIR LUCK FILE INTO THE GOLDEN EAGLE CASINO ON THE KICKAPOO INDIAN RESERVATION. (AP WIDE WORLD, STEVE ZUK)

MAYETTA

The Potawatomi resisted settlement in northern Indiana and western Michigan for 50 years, joining campaigns against the encroachers led by Pontiac, Little Turtle and Tecumseh. Eventually, they were forced from their lands. Although a few hundred remained behind, a far greater number live in Oklahoma. The Kansas Potawatomi are regarded as more conservative culturally.

 Prairie Band Potawatomi Casino and Bingo. 16277 Q Road, twenty-five miles north of Topeka by way of U.S. 75. (913)966-2375.

WHITE CLOUD

The Iowa reservation lies on both sides of the Missouri River, in Kansas and Nebraska. The lands are shared with the Sac & Fox. The Iowa lived near the junction of the Platte and Missouri Rivers during the period of Western settlement but were forced to give up their lands in Nebraska.

Iowa Tribe Games. Thirty-five miles northwest of St. Joseph, Missouri. (913)595-3258.

Missouri

Gaming was introduced in Missouri in 1992. At that time, only blackjack and poker were allowed. Games of chance such as roulette and slot machines were introduced after voters passed an amendment in 1994. Currently, a gaming policy enacted by the state allows players to lose a maximum of $500 per cruise. There are stipulated times for boarding river boat casinos, even for wholly land-based riverboats. Lottery information can be obtained by contacting the Missouri State Lottery.

 Missouri State Lottery, 1823 Southridge Drive, Jefferson City 65102, (573)751-4050. Sales: $423 million. Proceeds: $132 million. 100% education.

CARUTHERSVILLE

This is one of the larger towns in the Missouri Bootheel. It is, in fact, the main reason why there is a Missouri Bootheel. The original boundary line was drawn up in 1818 so that this area would have belonged to Arkansas. But John Hardeman Walker, whose family lived on the site that would become Caruthersville, protested this decision so vigorously that the territorial government reversed itself and attached the segment of land between the St. Francis and Mississippi Rivers to Missouri. Walker may have been given this benefit as a tribute to his heartiness. The original town was virtually wiped out by the great New Madrid earthquake of 1811. But Walker stayed on, built a plantation and helped plant the town that became Caruthersville. It was named in honor of a local judge. The casino is located on the Mississippi riverfront.

Casino Aztar 777 E. 3rd Street, 103 miles north of Memphis, Tennessee by way of I-55 and I-155. Sunday to Thursday, 10 a.m.–2 a.m.; Friday and Saturday, open until 4 a.m. 455 slots, thir-

ty-eight video poker machines, roulette, blackjack, and craps. The Casino Aztar has two restaurants, Diamonds and Dealer's Choice, and the Sidelines Sports Lounge. (314)333-1000.

KANSAS CITY

One of the traditional jumping-off points for the great westward trek, Kansas City grew up as the financial center and market for a vast cattle-raising and grain area. This is where the wagon trains headed out on the Santa Fe and Oregon Trails in the 1840s, leaving the familiar behind for a new life on the frontier. It was economically crippled by the battle for Kansas in the 1850s, as murderous pro– and anti–slavery forces rampaged across the area. Then the Civil War itself divided Missouri in half and Quantrill's Raiders devastated this area on behalf of the Confederacy.

Kansas City rebounded as a rail center. It would be immortalized as the place where bug-eyed cowboys went to see that "everything's up

A FIRE EATER (LEFT) ENTERTAINS GUESTS IN FRONT OF THE STATION CASINO IN KANSAS CITY. GUESTS (RIGHT) ARRIVE AT THE PRE-OPENING RECEPTION. (AP WIDE WORLD, CLIFF SCHIAPPA)

to date." Later on, it would be one of the birthplaces of the baseball's Negro Leagues, as well as swing and bebop, as a succession of great black musicians made the place their home. That segment of its past can be explored at the new Negro Leagues Baseball Museum, which recounts the history of segregated baseball before Jackie Robinson broke the color bar in 1947. Its river heritage is on view at The Arabia Steamboat Museum, which preserves the actual cargo of a Missouri river boat which sunk in 1856.

North Kansas City was a planned community, laid out as an industrial suburb in 1912. Riverside is located just across the Missouri River from the Kansas portion of Kansas City.

Argosy Casino, located off Missouri 9, east of the exit from I-635, eight miles north of downtown Kansas City, Kansas, in Riverside, Missouri. (816)746-7711. Sunday to Thursday, 8 a.m.–midnight; open until 2 a.m. Friday and Saturday. Boarding every two hours. 710 slots, thirty-two blackjack tables, six craps tables, 192 video poker machines, six poker tables, six caribbean stud poker tables, twenty-three video keno machines, six video blackjack machines, big six, roulette, bacarrat, and pai gow poker. Guests can relax in the Sidelines Sports Bar or grab a bite to eat in the Winner's Row and River Street Buffet restaurants.

Flamingo Hilton Casino Front Street exit of the I-35 bridge, on the south side of the Missouri River. (816)855-7777. Boarding every two hours, 8 a.m.–3 a.m.

Harrah's North Kansas City Casino, 1 Riverboat Drive, exit 6 of I-35, four miles north of downtown, in North Kansas

THE SIGN FOR THE RIVERPORT CASINO CENTER IN MARYLAND HEIGHTS, MISSOURI. (AP WIDE WORLD, TIM NORDMANN)

City. (816)472-7777. Daily, 8 a.m.–2 a.m. 968 slots including video poker machines, fifty-two blackjack tables, sixteen video keno machines, eight craps tables, eight caribbean stud poker tables, seven poker tables, roulette, baccarat, big six, and video blackjack. Guests can enjoy dining at the Fresh Market Buffet, One-Eyed Jack's Steaks & Seafood, North Star Deli and Winning Streak Sports Grill.

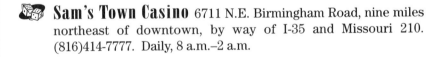 **Sam's Town Casino** 6711 N.E. Birmingham Road, nine miles northeast of downtown, by way of I-35 and Missouri 210. (816)414-7777. Daily, 8 a.m.–2 a.m.

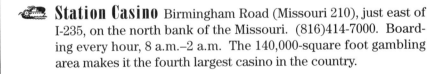 **Station Casino** Birmingham Road (Missouri 210), just east of I-235, on the north bank of the Missouri. (816)414-7000. Boarding every hour, 8 a.m.–2 a.m. The 140,000-square foot gambling area makes it the fourth largest casino in the country.

MARYLAND HEIGHTS

This area is known as Riverport, located immediately across the Missouri River from St. Charles. The two casinos, which opened early in 1997, are next to the Riverport Amphitheater. There is also an adjacent hotel.

 Harrah's Casino St. Louis. Located off I-70, just east of the Missouri River bridge. Daily, 8 a.m.–4 a.m., with boardings on the hour. (314)770-8100.

 Players Casino. Located off I-70, just east of the Missouri River bridge. Daily, 8 a.m.–4 a.m., with boardings on the hour. (314)432-8255.

ST. CHARLES

The bluffs that rise here are the first high ground along the Missouri as it heads westward from the Mississippi River. The French considered it a natural place for settlement and they called it Les Petites Cotes (Little Hills.) The name was changed to San Carlos when the Spanish governed the area, then became the anglicized St. Charles after the Louisiana Purchase of 1803. This was where the Lewis and Clark Expedition rendezvoused to prepare for the historic exploration of the river. Among those who came to settle near the wilderness outpost was Daniel Boone, fed up by the encroachments of civilization in his old Kentucky home. It was Missouri's first state capital and preserves the original State House, seat of government from 1821–26. In recent years, the town has been drawn into the suburban orbit of Greater St. Louis.

 Station Casino. Off the Fifth Street exit of I-70 and then east to the Missouri riverfront. Twenty-two miles northwest of St. Louis. Gaming on both a riverboat and a barge. Daily, 9 a.m.–1 a.m. on the riverboat with boarding on the odd hours; 10 a.m.–2 a.m. on the barge with boarding on the even hours. (314)949-7777.

ST. JOSEPH

The Pony Express galloped towards California from the stables of St. Joseph. At one time, its most prominent citizen was a Mr. Howard; who, in reality, was the legendary outlaw Jesse James. He was shot down in his home here in 1882 by a reward-seeking former associate. The town grew up as a trading post on the Missouri River in 1827. It was the last settlement westward-bound travelers passed as they headed up the big river and mountain men walked its streets with the pelts they had brought east to trade. The city has a fine collection of Victorian mansions built during this era. It also preserved many landmarks of the old frontier, including the original Pony Express stables; houses built by the town's founder, Joseph Robidoux, and Jesse James' home.

THE STATION CASINO IN ST. CHARLES, MISSOURI. ABOUT THIRTY-FIVE MILLION PEOPLE WILL PULL SLOTS, TOSS THE DICE AND PLAY CARDS ON GAMBLING BOATS THIS YEAR, MAKING IT MISSOURI'S NUMBER ONE TOURIST ATTRACTION. (AP WIDE WORLD, LEON ALGEE)

St. Jo Frontier Casino 77 Francis Street and Riverfront Park, off exit 6 of I-229. Sunday to Thursday, 8 a.m.–3 a.m.; Friday and Saturday, open until 5 a.m. (816)279-7577.

ST. LOUIS

Of all the riverboats along the Mississippi, The Admiral is docked on the most historic ground. It adjoins the Jefferson National Expansion Memorial, the soaring monument to America's move West. For decades this was the gateway to the middle border, the largest city in the West, and the trade of a continent flowed past its doors. The city grew up along the riverfront as a French fur trading outpost but became

MICHAEL WEBER, A BLACKJACK DEALER ON THE PRESIDENT CASINO ON THE ADMIRAL, DEALS THE CARDS TO THE PLAYERS. (AP WIDE WORLD, TIM NORDMANN)

nationally important after the Louisiana Purchase as the entry point to the new western lands. After the gateway shifted farther West, St. Louis continued to grow as a manufacturing center. In the words of one song it was famous for "shoes, booze and the St. Louis Blues." One of its best years was 1904, when the great World's Fair here gave the world its first hot dog, first ice cream cone, third Olympic Games and the enduring song "Meet Me in St. Louis, Louis."

Plans for reclaiming the riverfront as a historic district date back to the 1930s. But it took thirty years for land acquisition and construction to be completed. The Gateway Arch, designed by Eero Saarinen and topped off in 1965, is one of the most readily identifiable civic symbols in the world. Under the arch itself is the excellent Museum of Westward Expansion. Just to the north, and adjacent to the riverboat, is Laclede's Landing. A dining and entertainment district, it is situated on Pierre Laclede's original trading post of 1764. The area preserves some of the city's finest commercial structures from the nineteenth century.

President Casino on The Admiral. Off the Sixth Street exit of I-70, at the foot of Washington Ave., just north of the Gateway Arch. (800)878-4711. Daily, 8 a.m.–2 a.m., boarding every other hour. 1,410 slots, thirty-two blackjack tables, four craps

The National Bowling Hall of Fame

More than three hundred types of bowling have been traced to France, and since St. Louis is a city heavily influenced by French and German traditions, the sport was always popular here. The Women's International Bowling Congress was founded in the city in 1917 and Budweiser, which is based locally, has been a sponsor of some of the most formidable teams in the sport's history. So when cities were invited to bid for the Bowling Hall of Fame in 1978, St. Louis came up with a free piece of land downtown and was awarded the facility.

There are historical displays here, the most popular being an old fashioned alley with hand set pins. There are also exhibits of vintage equipment, memorablia of some of the sport's greatest figures, and a video show in which top bowlers offer tips to the viewer.

The museum is located directly across from Busch Stadium, at 111 Stadium Plaza. It is open daily, 9–7, Memorial Day to Labor Day. During the rest of the year, it is open Monday through Saturday, 9–5, and Sunday, 12–5. Admission is $5.00 for adults and $3.00 for children. Call (314)231-6340 for more information. (From *Pop Culture Landmarks: A Traveler's Guide*, by George Cantor, Visible Ink Press, 1995)

tables, nineteen poker tables, twenty-two video keno machines, roulette, baccarat, and video blackjack. The Admiral offers dining in the Four Aces Food Court and in the St. Louie Restaurant.

SENECA

Oklahoma's tribal gaming laws permit only Bingo, so this facility was placed a few steps across the state line to allow for a wider range of casino games. The Eastern Shawnee, highly assimilated into the general population, are scattered throughout adjacent Ottawa County, Oklahoma.

 Border Town Casino, *(Eastern Shawnee Tribe of Oklahoma).* Twenty miles south of Joplin, on Missouri 43. (918)666-8702.

Nebraska

Gaming in Nebraska includes placing bets at the track and a Native American casino. For information regarding the lottery, contact the Nebraska State Lottery.

 Nebraska State Lottery, 301 Centennial Mall South, 2nd Floor, Lincoln 68509, (402)471-6100. Sales: $82 million. Proceeds: $24 million. 49.5% education; 25% environment; 24.5% solid waste landfill closure; 1% Compulsive Gamblers Assistance Fund.

GRAND ISLAND

 Fonner Park, thoroughbred track. At 700 E. Stolley Park Road. (308)382-4515. February–April.

VALENTINE

The Teton were the westernmost and most populous branch of the Sioux during the eighteenth century. Leadership during the long campaign against the U.S. Army on the Northern Plains in the 1860s and 70s was drawn from this part of the tribe. The Rosebud Reservation was set up for the Brule and Two Kettle sub-tribes as part of the 1889 realignment of Sioux land into five disconnected portions. The reservation itself lies across the South Dakota border, but Nebraska has licensed this casino.

 Rosebud Casino, *(Rosebud Sioux Tribe).* Eighty miles south of I-90, at Murdo, S.D., on U.S. 83. (605)378-3800.

North Dakota

North Dakota law allows for charitable gaming in addition to casinos on approved Native American reservations. Native American casinos are allowed to operate slot machines, but charitable gaming operations are not. Charitable gaming operations offer blackjack or poker inside restaurants, bars and taverns. A percentage of the profits made from the tables goes to the affiliated charity. The State Attorney General enforces strict guidelines, monitoring how the charity organization uses the profits.

BELCOURT

The Chippewa are usually associated with woodland areas, but some of them pushed as far west as the plains of North Dakota. They participated, along with the Cree, in the Riel Rebellion, which sought to detach the Manitoba area from Canada. Afterwards, they were assigned to reservations on both side of the frontier, with the American Chippewa going to Turtle Mountain.

 Wild Rose Casino, *(Turtle Mountain Band of Chippewa).* Highway 5 West, one-hundred-fifteen miles northeast of Minot, by way of North Dakota 5, 3 and U.S. 2. (701)477-3340.

FORT YATES

The Standing Rock Reservation spreads across both North and South Dakota, along the western bank of the Missouri River. This is where most of the Hunkpapa band of western Sioux, of which Sitting Bull was a leader, settled. This was also his burial place for sixty-three years, until his remains were removed to Mobridge, South Dakota when it was feared a new dam might inundate the site. The reservation was whittled down from its original four million acres to the present 875,000

The Norsk Hostfest

In the first three decades of the twentieth century, North Dakota had the highest percentage of foreign-born rural population in America. One-third of them traced their roots to Norway. For a time, Norwegian Independence Day, May 17, marking Norway's independence from Sweden and Denmark, was observed as a state holiday.

Over the years, that sense of connection with the old country had weakened. But most of North Dakota's cities still have large Norwegian populations. Minot, which began as a Great Northern Railroad camp site in 1887, grew up just as the wave of Norse immigration was peaking. Its Norsk Hostfest celebrates all the Scandinavian cultures, but the emphasis is on the heritage of Norway. The celebration takes place the second week in October at the State Fairgrounds in Minot and includes traditional Scandinavian music, dancing, crafts, and food. For more information, contact the Norsk Hostfest Offices, P.O. Box 1347, Minot 58702, (701)852-2368. (From *Historic Festivals: A Traveler's Guide*, by George Cantor, Visible Ink Press, 1996)

acres. The standing rock for which the reservation is named, carried from one settlement to another by the Hunkpapa, occupies a place of honor overlooking the Missouri.

 Prairie Knights Casino, *(Standing Rock Sioux Tribe)*. Sixty-five miles south of Bismarck by way of North Dakota 6 and 24. (701)854-7777.

HANKINSON

The reservation is inhabited by two branches of the Santee, or Eastern Sioux, who were forced from Minnesota after the uprising of 1862. They also operate a casino just across the South Dakota line.

 Dakota Magic Casino, *(Sisseton-Wahpeton Sioux Tribe)*. Sixty miles south of Fargo, by way of I-29 and North Dakota 11. (701)242-7559.

MINOT

The Minot Hockey Boosters receives money from the gaming operations at the International Inn.

International Inn, *(charitable gaming operation).* Located at 1505 North Broadway. (701)852-3161. Six blackjack tables.

NEW TOWN

The Three Affiliated Tribes are the Mandan, Hidatsa and Arikara. All were agricultural peoples who lived along the Missouri and were placed in this reservation in 1870. When their former townsite was wiped out in the construction of Garrison Dam in 1954, a planned community was created for them. That is why it is called New Town. The three tribes have created a successful tourism industry in this lake country and the Four Bears Bridge across the river is one of the scenic highlights of the area.

 Four Bears Casino, *(Three Affiliated Tribes of the Fort Berthold Reservation).* Seventy-five miles southwest of Minot, by way of North Dakota 23 and U.S. 83. (701)627-4343.

SPIRIT LAKE

The Fort Totten reservation was set up in 1867 to house the Sioux who had fled Minnesota after the uprising earlier in the decade. It is situated in a beautiful spot, on the southern shore of Devils Lake. The reservation also contains the Sully's Hill Game Preserve, a refuge for buffalo and elk.

 Spirit Lake Casino, *(Devils Lake Sioux Tribe).* One-hundred miles west of Grand Forks, by way of U.S. 2 and North Dakota 57. (800)946-8238. 458 slots, ten blackjack tables, craps, five poker tables, twenty-five keno seats, and a 510-seat Bingo hall, which features daily regular and early-bird sessions.

Oklahoma

Oklahoma law currently permits only bingo under the terms of its gaming compact with the state's tribes. There are now thirty-three such operations. Because of the unique features of Native American life in Oklahoma, in which there are no reservations and tribes still inhabit the areas they were assigned when it was the Indian Territories, listings in this section are given under the headings of tribes rather than by cities. Racetracks are listed at the end of the chapter.

APACHE NATION

Most members of the Apache were settled on reservations in Arizona and New Mexico. But a small group of Chiricahua, from New Mexico, chose to move here. The city was a major tribal administrative center during territorial days and is home to the American Indian Exposition, the third week of every August.

 Na-I-Sha Games, in Anadarko, 620 E. Colorado Street. Sixty-three miles southwest of Oklahoma City, by way of I-44 and U.S. 62. (405)247-9331.

CHEROKEE NATION

Oklahoma was the end of the Trail of Tears for the Cherokee in the 1830s, a forced march from their former homes in Georgia and Tennessee on which one-quarter of the tribe perished. A skilled and literate people, the Cherokee rebuilt their lives and prosperity in their new homes and are the most populous group in northeastern Oklahoma. The government edifices of the Cherokee National capital are in Tahlequah, including the Supreme Court and Capitol buildings. It is one of the most historic Native American communities in the country. There is also an excellent Cherokee Heritage Center in this onetime capital.

Bingo Outposts of Catoosa, Roland, Siloam Springs.
Catoosa is at the northeastern edge of Tulsa, by way of I-44 and
Oklahoma 66. Roland is off I-40, just across the line from Fort
Smith, Arkansas. Siloam Springs is on U.S. 412, across the line
from Siloam Springs, Arkansas. The administrative center for all
three casinos is in the Cherokee capital of Tahlequah, (918)458-
7611. The United Keetoowah Band of Cherokees operate their
own casino in Tahlequah, thirty miles northeast of Muskogee, on
U.S. 62. (918)456-6131.

CHEYENNE AND ARAPAHO NATION

Both of these tribes were arbitrarily split into northern and
southern divisions and moved to Oklahoma by the federal government.
Eventually, however, the government relented because of the hardship
in adjusting to new climatic conditions. Reservations were established
for the northern Cheyenne in Montana and the northern Arapaho in
Wyoming. The two southern groups of the two tribes are closely associated in western Oklahoma.

 Clinton High Stakes Bingo, in Clinton is at the U.S. 183
exit of I-40, eighty-seven miles west of Oklahoma City. (405)323-
5640.

 Lucky Star Bingo, in Concho is north of I-40, on U.S. 81, thirty-five miles west of Oklahoma City. (405)262-7612.

 Watonga Bingo in Watonga is on U.S. 281, north of I-40, seventy miles northwest of Oklahoma City. (405)623-9299.

CHICKASAW NATION

The Chickasaw were removed to Oklahoma from ancestral lands
in western Kentucky and Tennessee. They engaged in agriculture here
and were strong supporters of the Confederacy, losing much of their
western lands after the Civil War as a result. There is a Chickasaw Cultural Center in Ada.

 The Gaming Center, in Ada at 1500 N. Country Club, is ninety miles southeast of Oklahoma City by way of I-40 and U.S. 377.
Ada is the administrative center of the Chickasaw. (405)436-
4113.

 The Goldsby Gaming Center, in Norman is off I-35, on the
southern outskirts of Oklahoma City. (405)436-4113.

Sulphur Gaming Center and Chickasaw Motor Inn, in Sulphur, is eighty-three miles south of Oklahoma City, by way of I-35 and Oklahoma 7. (405)622-2156.

 Touso Ishto Gaming, in Thackerville, is just west of 1-35 at the Texas border. (405)276-4229.

CHOCTAW NATION

The Choctaw, who came from Mississippi, were the most numerous native group in southeastern Oklahoma. About 17,000 tribal members live on individual landholdings in the area, while about one-quarter of that number remain in Mississippi.

 Choctaw Bingo-Arrowhead, in Canada, is in the Eufala Lake recreation area, off U.S. 69, fifty miles south of Muskogee. (800)422-2711.

 Choctaw Bingo Palace, in Durant, the tribal administrative center, is on U.S. 69, thirty miles north of Sherman, Texas. (405)920-0160.

 Choctaw Bingo Hall, in Idabel is on U.S. 70, forty-five miles east of the southernmost exit of the Indian Nation Parkway. (800)458-3682.

 Choctaw Bingo Hall, in Pocola is south of U.S. 271, just west of Fort Smith, Arkansas. (800)458-3682.

COMANCHE NATION

The Comanche lived in Oklahoma before it was designated as Indian Territory, although their numbers were swelled when the tribe was expelled from Texas after prolonged fighting in the 1840s. Fort Sill, the U.S. Army based originally built during the Indian Wars and later used to domicile various tribes, remains a major military installation and is located just north of Lawton.

 Comanche Nation Games, in Lawton, is eighty-five miles southwest of Oklahoma City, on I-44. (405)492-4982.

CREEK NATION

The Creek assumed a position of political leadership among the Five Civilized Tribes. Because of their central location in the Indian Ter-

The Ataloa Lodge

Bacone College is famous for its School of Indian Arts. The Ataloa Lodge on its campus in Muskogee was designed to show off works produced and contributed by graduates, students and benefactors. Among its collections of traditional and contemporary Native American art, the lodge houses one of the largest collections of Maria Martinez's San Indefonso pottery anywhere in the Southwest. An eighty-eight piece Kachina doll collection was recently added; the hand-carved pueblo dolls are given to children to help them identify dancers during tribal ceremonials. Ataloa also houses a large collection of Native American baskets from all parts of the North American continent. The museum is located on the northern edge of Muskogee at the intersection of U.S. 62 and Oklahoma 16. Open Monday–Friday, 10–4, with free admission. Call (918)683-4581 for more information. (From *North American Indian Landmarks: A Traveler's Guide,* by George Cantor, Visible Ink Press, 1993)

ritory, they were pivotal in the effort to establish a confederation, a system similar to their own tribal government. Okmulgee was the Creek capital and the Council House, built in 1878, was the scene of many historic political gatherings in the late nineteenth century. Muskogee, the administrative center for the Five Civilized Tribes, is the home of a museum that traces the histories of these peoples who contributed so much to the character and history of Oklahoma.

Bristow Indian Bingo, at 121 W. Lincoln, is twenty-eight miles southwest of Tulsa, on I-44. (918)367-9168.

Checotah Bingo, at 830 N. Broadway, is twenty-five miles south of Muskogee, on U.S. 69. (918)473-5200.

Eufaula Bingo, at 806 W. Forest Avenue, is thirty-seven miles south of Muskogee, on U.S. 69. (918)689-9191.

Muskogee Bingo is at 3240 W. Peak Boulevard. (918)683-1825.

Okmulgee Bingo is at 1601 N. Wood Drive is forty miles south of Tulsa, on U.S. 75. (918)756-8400.

Tulsa Bingo is at 1616 E. 81st Street. (918)299-8518.

IOWA TRIBE OF OKLAHOMA

A small group of Iowa live near their onetime tribal allotments, although the majority of the tribes reside on reservations in Nebraska and Kansas. The tribe, pushed relentlessly southwest from its historical home in Iowa, was given and then forced to surrender a half dozen various reservations in the Plains states before coming here in the 1870s.

 Cimarron Bingo, in Perkins, is fifty-seven miles northeast of Oklahoma City, by way of I-35 and Oklahoma 33. (405)547-5352.

KAW NATION

Also known as the Kansa, this people lost their two million acre reservation in Kansas in 1873 and were removed to Osage territory in Oklahoma.

 Kaw Bingo Enterprise. Kaw City is on Kaw Lake, thirty-two miles east of I-35, by way of Oklahoma 11. (405)269-2552.

KIOWA TRIBE

The Kiowa tribe regarded Oklahoma as its home base before it became Indian Territory. They were known for the quality of their horses and allied with the Comanches on raids for the animals as far south as Mexico.

 Kiowa Bingo. Carnegie is ninety-six miles southwest of Oklahoma City, by way of I-40 and Oklahoma 58. (405)654-2300.

PONCA TRIBE

The Ponca are closely related to the Omaha, joining them on migrations over the centuries and then settling near them, along the Niobrara River of Nebraska. About 2,000 of them remain near their former tribal lands.

 Ponca Tribal Bingo, south of Ponca City on U.S. 177, 103 miles north of Oklahoma City by way of I-35 and U.S. 60. (405)465-0040.

The National Cowboy Hall of Fame and Museum

To much of the world, the cowboy is the figure that symbolizes America—the man of the frontier, unattached to tradition and authority, carrying the law in a side holster, always ready for action. The real era of the cowboy was very short. The great cattle drives lasted about two decades, from a few years after the Civil War to the mid-1880s, when technology and a run of harsh weather put an end to them. Real cowboys had lingered on for another century, performing rather unglamorous jobs on the vast cattle ranches of the West. Even more profoundly, they live on in the popular culture. Beginning with the very first feature length movie, *The Great Train Robbery,* images of the men of the West have pervaded American entertainment—its films, novels and music.

You'll find all of them in this museum. There are those who lived the historical realities of cowboy life and those who only depicted those realities—all the great stars, from Tom Mix to Roy Rogers to John Wayne. They're all assembled in this one-time frontier town in the Indian Territory, many of them represented by displays of their own western collections.

Perhaps the most moving segment of the museum is the famed sculpture, *End of the Trail.* The eighteen-foot high work by James Earl Fraser, depicting an exhausted Indian slumping on his pony, is shown off in its own hall. Art work by Frederic Remington and Charles M. Russell is also displayed.

The museum is located just off Interstate 35, at 1700 Northeast 63rd Street in Oklahoma City. From Memorial Day through Labor Day, the museum is open daily from 8:30 a.m.–6 p.m. September–May, the museum is open daily from 9 a.m.–5 p.m. Admission is $6.50 for adults, $5.50 for senior citizens, $3.25 for children ages 6–12, and free for children under the age of six. For more information call (405)478-2250. (From *Pop Culture Landmarks: A Traveler's Guide,* by George Cantor, Visible Ink Press, 1995)

POTAWATOMI TRIBE

This is the largest group of Potawatomi in the country, counting 11,000 members, most of whom live in the Shawnee area.

 Firelake Entertainment Center, 1901 S. Gordon Cooper Drive. Thirty-five miles east of Oklahoma City, on I-40. (405)273-2242.

SAC & FOX NATION

These two affiliated tribes were forced southwest from Wisconsin and Iowa in the mid-nineteenth century. Eventually, many of them returned to reservations in Iowa and Nebraska, but a small number chose to remain in this area.

 Foxfire, Inc. Located in Edmond, one of the northern suburbs of Oklahoma City, by way of U.S. 77. (918)968-4406.

SEMINOLE NATION

After decades of resistance against Americans in Florida, the Seminoles were transported to Oklahoma in the 1850s. There are more tribal members here than in Florida.

 Seminole Bingo. Sixty miles southeast of Oklahoma City, by way of I-40 and Oklahoma 99. (405)382-7920.

SENECA-CAYUGA TRIBE

Members of the Iroquois Confederacy, both of these tribes sided with the British during the American Revolution and consequently lost most of their lands in New York. Most of the Seneca remained there, but a portion joined with the Cayuga to live among the Delaware people in Ohio. Eventually, they were removed to the Indian Territories where a small group remains.

 Seneca-Cayuga Gaming Operation. Located in Miami, twenty-eight miles southwest of Joplin, Missouri. (918)542-6609.

SHAWNEE NATION

The Shawnee were the main force of resistance to white settlement of the Ohio Valley, carrying on a fierce campaign over the decades in West Virginia, Kentucky and Ohio. Forced to disperse after the defeat of Tecumseh in 1813, the tribe split into several segments. The largest made their way to the Canadian River in Oklahoma and became known as the Absentee Shawnee. The Loyal Shawnee, who had remained in the Ohio area and lived among the Seneca, were given land with that tribe in northeastern Oklahoma.

Thunderbird Entertainment Center, 15700 E. Highway 9, on the southern outskirts of Oklahoma City in Norman. (405)360-9270.

Loyal Shawnee Bingo. Fifty-eight miles northeast of Tulsa, on I-44 in Vinita. (918)256-6914.

OKLAHOMA CITY

Remington Park, thoroughbred track. South from I-44, at the Eastern Avenue exit, seven miles northeast of downtown. March–December. (405)424-1000.

TULSA

Fair Meadows, thoroughbred track. Expo Square. South from I-244 at the Yale Avenue exit, east of downtown. May–July. (918)743-7223.

South Dakota

Casino gambling in this state is limited to Native American reservations and the old mining town of Deadwood, where it has a long history. Games permitted are blackjack, slot machines, video poker and poker tables. Lottery information is available from the South Dakota State Lottery.

 South Dakota State Lottery. 207 E. Capitol, Suite 200, Pierre 57501, (605)773-5770. Sales: $30 million. Proceeds: $6.9 million. 80% General fund; 20% capital construction.

AGENCY VILLAGE

These were two of the tribes exiled from Minnesota after the uprising of 1862 and this reservation was set aside for them five years later. The reservation itself is in North Dakota with the casino situated just across the state line.

 Dakota Connection, *(Sisseton-Wahpeton Sioux Tribe).* Off I-29, seventy-five miles north of Watertown. (605)698-4273.

DEADWOOD

The most famous poker game in American history was played in Deadwood. The Black Hills gold that created the town led to one of the most controversial battles the U.S. Army ever fought. The colorful figures of the Old West walked its streets, drank in its saloons, bet in its gaming halls. A great newspaper fortune was established nearby. It is the stuff of countless Western movies and legends. If ever a place seemed destined for casinos, it was Deadwood.

Tribal Gaming

Some of the more fortunate tribal groups refer to it as "the new buffalo." Casinos have become that important as a way of life among Native Americans in many parts of the country. Foxwoods, in Connecticut, is the largest casino in the Western Hemisphere, and the nearby Mohegan Sun casino is only slightly smaller. Large-scale gaming facilities have also been created in Michigan, Minnesota, Wisconsin and the Dakotas. But smaller casinos and bingo operations are more the norm among the tribes.

All of these facilities date from 1988, when President Ronald Reagan signed the Indian Gaming Regulatory Act. The legislation stipulates that federally registered tribes may open gaming operations after signing an agreement, or compact, with the state in which they are located. Many of the more succesful tribes have plowed profits into the reservation community to improve educational and health facilities. In some instances, schooling through graduate school and all medical expenses are being fully paid. However, bitter disputes also have broken out among tribal leaderships over eligibility for casino profits and residence requirements. Some states also have started taking tribal leaders to court, claiming that casinos have gone far beyond the scope of the compacts in terms of size, hours and expansion into off-reservation locations.

Time seems to have stopped here in America's centennial year, 1876. It was then that gold fever burned its brightest in Deadwood. That was the year Wild Bill Hickok, part-time lawman and full-time gambler, was shot in the back while holding aces and eights, which forever afterwards has been called the "dead man's hand." He was gunned down by a miner named Jack McCall. Some say McCall just wanted credit for killing a famous gunman. Others insist that he was put up to the deed by the town's lawless element (which may have constituted a clear majority). They feared that Hickok would be named marshal. Although acquitted by a kangaroo court, McCall was later rearrested, taken to the territorial capital of Yankton, tried and duly hanged. His complaint of double jeopardy was dismissed because the previous court was ruled to have no jurisdiction.

This was the same year in which, several miles to the northwest, General George A. Custer's command was annihilated at the Little Big Horn. The birth of Deadwood and Custer's death are part of the same story. Custer led a U.S. Army mapping expedition into the Native American territory of the Black Hills in 1874. That was, at least, its intended purpose. But one of the civilians on the trek found gold in French Creek, near the present town of Custer. The Army managed to hold back the flood of treasure-seekers for a little while. But the following year, the government changed its policy and allowed the miners in. The outraged tribes, to whom the land was sacred and guaranteed by treaty, immediately rose in revolt. An unprecedented coalition of Plains tribes began raiding throughout the area. Custer was sent into Montana to stop this activity—with fatal results for him.

The mining camp that started all this trouble was short-lived. In March, 1876, news of a strike in Deadwood Gulch made its way to Custer. According to contemporary reports, the population of Custer dropped overnight from 7,000 to 100. The other 6,900 went to Deadwood. Before the end of summer they were joined by about 18,000 companions. Many of them, sooner rather than later, wound up in Mount Moriah Cemetery, one of the busiest burial grounds in the West. Next to Hickok is the grave of Martha Jane Burke, known to folklore as Calamity Jane. In recent years, she has been depicted as a proto-feminist, a woman who held her own in a mean, man's world. Contemporary reports, however, indicate that she was regarded as mildly eccentric and if there was ever a romance between her and Hickok it was pretty much in her own imagination. When she died in 1903, she was given the grandest funeral in the town's history and her dying wish to be buried beside Wild Bill was honored.

The Homestake Mine in the neighboring town of Lead is the richest deposit of gold ever found in the United States. It was chartered in 1877 and one of the founding investors was George Hearst, of San Francisco. With his earnings, he was able to leave a $7 million inheritance to his son, William Randolph. He used it to launch a newspaper empire that changed the course of both American journalism and history.

Then as now, Main Street was the center of fun in Deadwood. Gambling was, in fact, legal in the town until 1946. Deadwood had the reputation, even then, of being a wide open place. When legalized gambling returned, forty-seven years later, it was in a far more sedate version. But every year Deadwood remembers its wild past with a community celebration, Days of '76, held on the first full weekend of August. "The Trial of Jack McCall," a re-enactment of the assassin's court proceedings, is put on every night but Sunday during the summer at the Old Town Hall. Old Time Saloon Number 10, at 657 Main Street, where the fatal shooting occurred, is a museum of the times. The Adams Memorial Museum, at Sherman and Deadwood Streets, is a more formal recapitulation of Deadwood's explosive past.

Deadwood is forty-one miles northwest of Rapid City, by way of I-90 and U.S. 14. There are ninety-five casinos, most of them small and concentrated along the 500-600 blocks of Main Street. They are open daily, twenty-four hours. Games offered are blackjack, slots, poker

tables and video poker. The average Deadwood casino contains about 100 slots, four blackjack tables and two poker tables.

🎲 **The Bullock,** in an historic hotel, at 633 Main Street. (605)578-1745.

🎲 **The Dakota Territory,** at 653 Main Street, features a collection of historic slots and gambling equipment, many of them associated with Deadwood's past. (605)578-3566. Thirty-two slot machines, video poker, blackjack and poker.

🎲 **The Franklin Hotel and Gambling Hall,** built in 1903, is at 700 Main Street. (605)578-2241.

🎲 **Gold Dust,** at 688 Main Street, (605)578-2100.

🎲 **Golddigger's Hotel and Gambling,** at 629 Main Street. (605)578-3213.

🎲 **Midnight Star,** at 677 Main Street, (605)578-1555. Features memorabilia from the making of the film "Dances with Wolves," which was shot in South Dakota. The Midnight Star offers the dining experiences of Jakes, located on the top of the casino, and Diamond Lil's Sports Bar & Grill. Fifty-six slots, video poker, blackjack, ten video keno machines, ten video blackjack machines.

🎲 **The Mineral Palace,** at 601 Main Street, is a modern hotel built in the Old West style. (605)578-2036.

🎲 **Wild Bill's Bar,** at 608 Main Street. (605)578-2177.

EAGLE BUTTE

This reservation on the west bank of the Missouri was set aside for five small divisions of the Western Sioux, or Teton branch of the tribe. These groups ranged between the river and the Black Hills. It was the invasion of their lands by miners in the 1870s that led to the confrontation with General George Custer's forces at the Little Big Horn.

 **C.R.S.T. Bingo,** *(Cheyenne River Sioux Tribe).* On U.S. 212, fifty miles west of the Missouri River bridge. (605)964-8910.

FLANDREAU

The majority of Native Americans in this area are from the Mdewakanton branch of the eastern, or Santee Sioux. They were exiled from Minnesota in the 1860s and left their reservation in Nebraska a decade later to settle here, just across the line from their former homes.

 Royal River Casino, *(Flandreau Santee Sioux).* Forty-five miles north of Sioux Falls, by way of I-29 and South Dakota 32. (605)997-3891.

FORT THOMPSON

The Yankton and Yanktonai division of the Sioux made up the middle branch of the tribe, between the Santee and Teton. They ranged along the Missouri River, from Iowa to the eastern half of the Dakotas. But disease and warfare eventually diminished their numbers and in the 1860s both tribes were resettled on Crow Creek.

 Lode Star Casino, *(Crow Creek Sioux Tribe).* Twenty-one miles north of I-90, by way of South Dakota 47. (605)245-2111.

LOWER BRULE

The Lower Brule were one of the most populous subdivisons of the Teton, or Western Sioux. Their lands run along the western bank of the Missouri River, an area that has been turned into a boating recreation area by the dams of the U.S. Army Corps of Engineers.

 Golden Buffalo Casino, *(Lower Brule Sioux Tribe).* Eighteen miles north of I-90, by way of North Dakota 47 and reservation roads. (605)473-5577.

MCLAUGHLIN

The Standing Rock Sioux also operate a casino across the state line, at Fort Yates, North Dakota.

 Bear Soldier Bingo, *(Standing Rock Sioux Tribe).* Twenty-five miles west of the Missouri River bridge on U.S. 12. (605)823-4364.

MOBRIDGE

This is a recreational area formed by the damming of the Missouri River to form Lake Oahe. This is also the burial site of Sitting Bull, moved here from Fort Yates, North Dakota, in 1953.

The Corn Palace Festival

When the citizens of Mitchell inquired how much it would take to hire John Philip Sousa's band to play for a week, his manager told them that they couldn't afford it. They persisted. $7,000, Sousa's representative wired back, thinking that would stop the nonsense. In 1904, that was more than most musicians made in a year. But Mitchell guaranteed that amount, even delivering it in cash to a dubious Sousa when he arrived by train.

The appearance of the renowned bandmaster, and the publicity he received for performing in this far-flung outpost for a solid week, elevated the Corn Palace Festival into an major American event. It had started in 1892 as a way for civic boosters to get Mitchell some publicity and show off the richness of its soil. The town was then and remains at the center of the Midwest's most productive corn belt. The farms of eastern South Dakota pace the country in terms of productivity.

The Corn Palace started out as a rather plain building that was easily adorned. But the present structure, a Moorish fantasy of domes and minarets, is covered with some 3,000 bushels of corn and grass in the harvest season. Much of it is dyed and arranged to form designs, with each festival having a different theme. During the rest of the year, the Palace, which seats about 4,500 people, is used for civic and athletic functions. The Corn Palace Festival offers name entertainment, a carnival, agricultural displays and demostrations. Mitchell is on Interstate 90, about seventy miles west of Sioux Falls. For more festival information, contact the Mitchell Chamber of Commerce, 604 North Main, Mitchell 57301, (605)996-7311. (From *Historic Festivals: A Traveler's Guide,* by George Cantor, Visible Ink Press, 1996)

 Grand River Casino, *(Standing Rock Sioux).* West on U.S. 12, 113 miles north of Pierre, by way of U.S. 83 and 12. (605)845-7104.

OELRICHS

 Prairie Wind Casino, *(Oglala Sioux).* East on U.S. 18, thirty-five miles east of Hot Springs. (605)535-6300.

PINE RIDGE

Pine Ridge is the largest reservation in South Dakota, and exceeded in population only by the Navajo tract in the Southwest. The

Oglala Sioux were the most populous branch of the Teton, or Western Sioux, and much of that tribe's leadership, including Crazy Horse and Red Cloud, was drawn from the group.

The climactic tragedy in relations between Native Americans and whites was played out here at Wounded Knee. The site of the 1890 massacre is just a few miles north of the administrative center at Pine Ridge. There is also a museum of Oglala culture here.

 Children's Village Bingo, *(Oglala Sioux Tribe).* On U.S. 18, sixty-five miles east of Hot Springs. (605)867-5821.

WAGNER

The Yankton, or middle branch of the Sioux, operate another casino at the Crow Creek Reservation. Wagner is located in a recreational area, just east of the Missouri River and Fort Randall Dam.

 Fort Randall Casino, *(Yankton Sioux Tribe).* West Highway 46, sixty-five miles southwest of Mitchell, by way of South Dakota 37 and U.S. 18. (605)487-7871.

WATERTOWN

This is an off-reservation site run by this Eastern Sioux people, one of two they have in the state.

 Dakota Sioux Casino, *(Sisseton-Wahpeton Sioux Tribe).* 16415 Sioux Conifer Rd. (605)882-2051.

Texas

Gaming in Texas is limited to betting at the race tracks and one Indian casino in El Paso, The Speaking Rock Casino, which opened in 1995. State lottery information can be obtained by contacting the Texas State Lottery.

 Texas State Lottery, 611 E. Sixth Street, Austin 78701, (512)344-5000. Sales: $3.4 billion. Proceeds: $1.1 billion. 100% General fund.

EL PASO

One of the New Mexico pueblos stayed loyal to Spain during the insurrection of 1680. The Tigua accompanied the retreating soldiers to El Paso and established a new pueblo there. Ysleta is where they have remained for 300 years, cut off from their brethren in the north. It is the oldest continuously-inhabited community on Texas soil. (If the Rio Grande had not shifted its course several years ago, however, it would be in Mexico.) There is a mission as old as the pueblo here as well as a museum of Tigua culture.

 Speaking Rock Casino, *(Ysleta Del Sur Pueblo).* Fourteen miles east of the city, by way of I-10. 122 S. Old Pueblo Road. (915)858-6934. Open Monday–Sunday, 1 p.m.–4 a.m. Speaking Rock Casino offers a style of blackjack called Tigua 21. The game consists of a banker and players, with the casino collecting a small commission for each round of play. Players can act as the banker and pay off the winning hands and collect all losing bets. The house supplies a dealer who deals the cards to the players and collects the commission for the house. There are sixteen Tigua 21 tables. Poker, video poker machines and bingo are also available.

HOUSTON

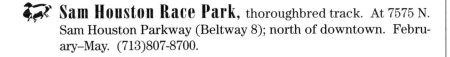 **Sam Houston Race Park,** thoroughbred track. At 7575 N. Sam Houston Parkway (Beltway 8); north of downtown. February–May. (713)807-8700.

MANOR

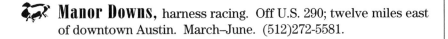 **Manor Downs,** harness racing. Off U.S. 290; twelve miles east of downtown Austin. March–June. (512)272-5581.

SAN ANTONIO

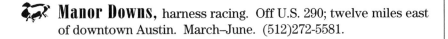 **Retama Park,** thoroughbred track. Off I-35 at the Selma exit, just north of Loop 1604; northeast of downtown. May–November. (210)651-7000.

WEST PACIFIC

Alaska
Arizona
California
Colorado
Idaho
Montana
Nevada
New Mexico
Oregon
Washington
Wyoming

Alaska

1. Metlakatla Indian Community Bingo, Metlakatla

Arizona

2. Cliff Castle Casino, Camp Verde
3. Fort McDowell Gaming Center, Fountain Hills
4. Lone Butte Casino, Chandler
5. Harrah's Ak-Chin Casino, Maricopa
6. Blue Water Casino, Parker
7. Mazatzal Casino, Payson
8. Turf Paradise, Phoenix
9. Bucky's Casino, Prescott
10. Prescott Downs, Prescott
11. Yavapai Bingo, Prescott
12. Wild Horse Pass Casino, Sacaton
13. Apache Gold Casino, San Carlos
14. Cocopah Bingo, Somerton
15. Casino of the Sun, Tucson
16. Desert Diamond Casino, Tucson
17. Hon Dah Casino, Whiteriver

California

18. Golden Gate Fields, Albany
19. Viejas Casino and Turf Club, Alpine
20. Mono Wind Casino, Auberry
21. Santa Anita, Arcadia
22. Sierra Spring Casino, Big Pine
23. Cache Creek Bingo and Casino, Brooks
24. Pit River Casino, Burney
25. Casino Morongo, Cabazon
26. Spotlight 29 Casino, Coachella
27. Colusa Indian Bingo, Colusa
28. Elk Valley Casino, Crescent City
29. Del Mar Thoroughbred Club, Del Mar
30. Sycuan Indian Bingo and Poker Casino, El Cajon
31. Table Mountain Rancheria Casino and Bingo, Friant
32. Havasu Landing Resort and Casino, Havasu
33. San Manuel Indian Bingo and Casino, Highland
34. Lucky Bear Casino and Bingo, Hoopa
35. Hopland Sho-ka-wah Casino, Hopland
36. Cabazon Bingo and Fantasy Springs Casino, Indio
37. Hollywood Park, Inglewood

38. Jackson Indian Bingo and Casino, Jackson
39. Chicken Ranch Bingo, Jamestown
40. Barona Casino and Bingo, Lakeside
41. Palace Indian Gaming Center, Lemoore
42. Los Alamitos Race Course, Los Alamitos
43. Robinson Racheria Bingo and Casino, Nice
44. Feather Falls Casino, Oroville
45. Gold Country Casino, Oroville
46. Spa Hotel and Casino, Palm Springs
47. Alameda County Fairgrounds, Pleasanton
48. Win-River Casino Bingo, Redding
49. Soboba Legends Casino, San Jacinto
50. Bay Meadows, San Mateo
51. Chumsah Casino, Santa Ynez
52. Northern Lights Casino, Susanville
53. Pechanga Entertainment Center, Temecula
54. Cher-Ae Heights Bingo and Casino, Trinidad
55. Paradise Casino, Winterhaven

Colorado

56. Arapaho Park, Aurora
57. Bronco Billy's II, Black Hawk
58. Bullwhackers, Black Hawk
59. Crooks Palace, Black Hawk
60. El Dorado Casino, Black Hawk
61. Gilpin Hotel Casino, Black Hawk
62. Gold Mine Casino, Black Hawk
63. Golden Canary, Black Hawk
64. Golden Gates Casino, Black Hawk
65. Jazz Alley Casino, Black Hawk
66. Lilly Belle's, Black Hawk
67. Otto's Casino, Black Hawk
68. Pick-a-Dilly Casino, Black Hawk
69. Baby Doe's Silver Dollar Casino, Central City
70. Bullwhacker's, Central City
71. Central Palace Casino, Central City
72. Dillon's Double Eagle, Central City
73. Golden Rose Casino, Central City
74. Harrah's Casino, Central City
75. Harvey's Wagon Wheel Casino, Central City
76. Long Branch Saloon and Casino, Central City
77. Teller House, Central City
78. Toll Gate Casino, Central City
79. Silver Slipper, Central City
80. Bronco Billy's, Cripple Creek

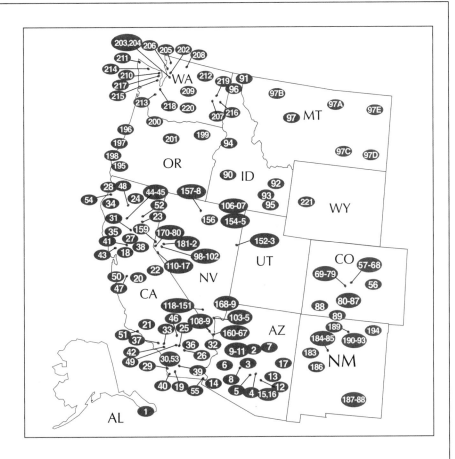

81. Gold Digger's Casino, Cripple Creek
82. Gold Rush Hotel and Casino, Cripple Creek
83. Legends, Cripple Creek
84. Bobby Womack's Gaming Parlor, Cripple Creek
85. Diamond Lil's, Cripple Creek
86. Midnight Rose Hotel and Casino, Cripple Creek
87. Imperial Hotel and Casino, Cripple Creek
88. Ute Mountain Casino, Cortez
89. Sky Ute Casino and Lodge, Ignacio

Idaho

90. Les Bois Park, Boise
91. Kootenai River Plaza, Boise
92. Teton Racing, Idaho Falls
93. Shoban Exit 80 Casino, Fort Hall
94. Clearwater River Casino, Lapwai

95. Pocatello Park at the Bannock County Fairgrounds, Pocatello
96. Coeur d'Alene Tribal Bingo, Worley

Montana

97. State Fair, thoroughbred track, Great Falls
97a. 4 C's Casino, Box Elder
97b. Blackfeet Bingo, Browning
97c. Absaloka Casino, Crow Agency
97d. Northern Cheyenne Social Club, Lame Deer
97e. Silverwolf Casino, Wolf Point

Nevada

98. Carson Nugget, Carson City
99. Cactus Jack's Casino, Carson City
100. Ormsby House, Carson City
101. Carson Horshoe, Carson City

102. Carson Station, Carson City
103. Gold Strike Hotel and Casino, Henderson
104. Nevada Palace Hotel and Casino, Henderson
105. Railroad Pass Hotel and Casino, Henderson
106. Cactus Pete's Resort Hotel and Casino, Jackpot
107. Horseshu Hotel and Casino, Jackpot
108. Primadonna Resort and Casino, Jean
109. Whiskey Pete's Hotel and Casino, Jean
110. Hyatt Regency Lake Tahoe Resort and Casino
111. Cal-Neva Lodge, Lake Tahoe
112. Crystal Bay Club, Lake Tahoe
113. Tahoe Biltmore Lodge, Lake Tahoe
114. Caesar's Tahoe, Lake Tahoe
115. Harrah's Lake Tahoe Resort and Casino
116. Harvey's Resort Hotel and Casino, Lake Tahoe
117. Horizon Casino Resort, Lake Tahoe
118. Sahara, Las Vegas
119. Circus Circus, Las Vegas
120. Riviera, Las Vegas
121. Sheraton Desert Inn, Las Vegas
122. Mirage, Las Vegas
123. Harrah's Las Vegas, Las Vegas
124. Flamingo Hilton, Las Vegas
125. Caesar's Palace, Las Vegas
126. Bally's Las Vegas, Las Vegas
127. Monte Carlo Resort, Las Vegas
128. MGM Grand, Las Vegas
129. Tropicana, Las Vegas
130. Excalibur, Las Vegas
131. Luxor, Las Vegas
132. New York, New York, Las Vegas
133. The Stardust, Las Vegas
134. Imperial Palace, Las Vegas
135. Barbary Coast, Las Vegas
136. Aladdin, Las Vegas
137. Hacienda, Las Vegas
138. Gold Coast, Las Vegas
139. Palace Station, Las Vegas
140. Maxim, Las Vegas
141. Las Vegas Hilton, Las Vegas
142. Rio Suites, Las Vegas
143. California, Las Vegas
144. Fitzgerald's, Las Vegas
145. Four Queens, Las Vegas
146. Fremont, Las Vegas
147. Golden Nugget, Las Vegas
148. Binion's Horseshoe, Las Vegas
149. Lady Luck, Las Vegas
150. Las Vegas Club, Las Vegas
151. Plaza, Las Vegas
152. Peppermill Inn and Casino, Wendover
153. Silver Smith Casino and Resort, Wendover
154. Four-Way Cafe and Casino, Wells
155. Nevade Travel Center and Casino, Wells
156. Red Lion Motor Inn and Casino, Elko
157. Jackpot Owl Club, Battle Mountain
158. Red Lion Inn and Casino, Winnemucca
159. The Boomtown Hotel and Casino, Verdi
160. Avi Hotel Casino, Laughlin
161. The Colorado Belle and Casino, Laughlin
162. Edgewater Hotel and Casino, Laughlin
163. Flamingo Hilton, Laughlin
164. Golden Nugget Casino, Laughlin
165. Harrah's Laughlin, Laughlin
166. Ramada Express, Laughlin
167. The Riverside Casino and Resort, Laughlin
168. Players Island Resort Spa, Mesquite
169. Virgin River Hotel and Casino, Mesquite
170. Bally's, Reno
171. Circus Circus, Reno
172. El Dorado Hotel and Casino, Reno
173. Flamingo Hilton, Reno
174. Harrah's, Reno
175. Atlantis Casino Resort, Reno
176. Club Cal-Neva, Reno
177. Fitzgerald's Hotel Casino, Reno
178. Peppermill Hotel and Casino, Reno
179. Riverboat Hotel and Casino, Reno
180. The Virginian, Reno
181. John Ascuaga's Nugget, Reno
182. Silver Club, Reno

New Mexico

183. Sky City Casino, Acomita
184. Isleta Gaming Palace, Albuquerque
185. Sandia Casino, Albuquerque
186. Santa Ana Star Casino, Bernalillo
187. Apache Nugget Casino, Dulce
188. Ruidoso Downs, Dulce
189. OHKAY Casino, San Juan
190. Camel Rock Casino, Santa Fe
191. Cities of Gold Casino, Santa Fe
192. The Downs at Santa Fe, Santa Fe

193. Sunland Park, Santa Fe
194. Taos Slot Room, Taos

Oregon

195. Seven Feathers Gaming Resort, Canyonville
196. Spirit Mountain Gaming, Grand Ronde
197. Chinook Winds, Lincoln City
198. The Mill Casino, North Bend
199. Wildhorse Gaming Resort, Pendleton
200. Portland Meadows, Portland
201. Indian Head Gaming Center, Warm Springs

Washington

202. Swinomish Casino, Anacortes
203. Emerald Downs, Auburn
204. Muckleshoot Indian Casino, Auburn
205. Lummi Casino, Bellingham
206. Harrah's Skagit Valley Casino
207. Two Rivers Casino, Davenport
208. Nooksack River Casino, Deming
209. Mill Bay Casino, Manson
210. Tulalip Bingo, Marysville
211. Makah Bingo, Neah Bay
212. Okanogan Bingo Casino, Okanogan
213. Chehalis Tribal Lucky Eagle Casino, Rochester
214. Seven Cedars Casino, Sequim
215. Little Creek Casino, Shelton
216. Playfair Racecourse, Spokane
217. Suquamish Bingo, Suquamish
218. Puyallup Tribes Bingo Palace, Tacoma
219. Spokane Indian Casino, Wellpinit
220. Yakima Meadows, Yakima

Wyoming

221. 789 Bingo, Fort Washakie

Alaska

This community was founded in 1887 when missionary William Duncan moved fifty Tsimshian tribe members from British Columbia after a disagreement with church authorities. The Annette Island reserve was established by Congress four years later.

 Metlakatla Indian Community Bingo, on Annette Island, across the inlet from Kethickan with regular ferry service. (907) 886-4447.

Arizona

Currently, Arizona does not allow state-run casinos. There are fourteen Native American casinos. For lottery informaton, contact the Arizona State Lottery.

 Arizona State Lottery, 4740 E. University, Phoenix 85034, (602) 921-4400. Sales: $259 million. Proceeds: $86 million. 39% General Fund; 27% Local Transportation Assistance Fund; 23% Heritage Fund; 9% County Assistance Fund; 2% Economic Development Fund.

CAMP VERDE

The Yavapai ranged across western Arizona in the nineteenth century and many of their bands became closely allied with the Apache in raids against neighboring tribes. They share the Camp Verde Reservation.

 Cliff Castle Casino *(Yavapai Apache Tribe)*. Fifty-five miles south of Flagstaff, by way of I-17 and Arizona 260. (520) 567-9704.

FOUNTAIN HILLS

This reservation was established as a separate entity for small bands of Mohave and Apache, who are culturally distinct from the other tribes who hold land in the Phoenix area. Built around an old Army base it now adjoins some of the richest resort property in the Southwest.

 Fort McDowell Gaming Center *(Fort McDowell Mohave-Apache Indian Community)*. In the eastern suburbs of Phoenix. (602) 837-1424.

THE EXTERIOR OF HARRAH'S AK-CHIN CASINO IN MARICOPA, ARIZONA. (COURTESY OF HARRAH'S AK-CHIN CASINO)

CHANDLER

The reservation is occupied by members of the Pima and Maricopa tribes. These are agricultural people whose ancestors created extensive irrigation systems and farmed the desert along the Gila and Salt Rivers on the present site of Phoenix. There is a museum of Gila culture at Sacaton.

 Lone Butte Casino *(Gila River Indian Reservation).* Both the Wild Horse Pass Casino in Scanton and the Lone Butte Casino are operated by the Gila River Indian Community. Lone Butte is at 1201 S. 56th Street, Chandler, in the southern suburbs of Phoenix, off I-10. (520) 796-7712.

MARICOPA

The Maricopa migrated to the Gila Valley in the sixteenth century from their former home along the Colorado River. They absorbed many smaller tribes in the area and were allied with the Pima, with whom they share reservation lands in this area.

153

Harrah's Ak-Chin Casino *(Ak-Chin Indian Community).* 15406 N. Maricopa Road. Thirty-five miles south of Phoenix, by way of I-10 and Arizona 347. (602) 802-5000

PARKER

The Colorado River reservation, located just across from California, is inhabited by the Mohave and Chemehuevi tribes. The Mohave have lived along the river for 200 years and the reservation was organized for them in 1865. When the Chemehuevi lands in California were flooded out in the construction of Parker Dam (part of the Los Angeles water system), that tribe joined the Mohave here. The area has been developed as a recreational boating center and a museum of the Colorado River Tribes is located in Parker.

 Blue Water Casino *(Colorado River Indian Tribes).* 119B W. Riverside Drive. Thirty-three miles south of Lake Havasu City, by way of Arizona 95. (520) 669-7777.

PAYSON

The Tonto were one of five bands of western Apache who came to Arizona in the early nineteenth century and became closely allied with the Navajo. Their small reservation is located among magnificent mountain scenery in the Tonto National Forest.

 Mazatzal Casino *(Tonto Apache Tribe).* Eighty miles northeast of Phoenix, by way of Arizona 87. (520) 474-6044.

PHOENIX

 Turf Paradise, thoroughbred track. Off I-17 from the Bell Road exit, then east to 19th Avenue, north of downtown Phoenix. October–mid-May. (602) 942-1101.

PRESCOTT

One of the early territorial capitals of Arizona, Prescott was built on the ancestral lands of the Yavapai. Their reservation lies just north of the city. This nomadic tribe was the strongest group in northwestern Arizona and regularly raided the agricultural peoples in the adjacent river valleys.

Bucky's Casino. Sheraton Hotel, north of town on Highway 69. (520) 776-1666.

 Prescott Downs. Thursday to Sunday, Memorial Day to Labor Day. (520) 445-0220.

 Yavapai Bingo *(Yavapai-Prescott Indian Tribe).* 530 E. Merritt Street. (520) 445-8790.

SACATON

The Gila River Reservation is occupied by members of the Pima and Maricopa tribes. There is a museum of Gila culture at Sacaton.

 Wild Horse Pass Casino, *(Gila River Indian Community).* Wild Horse Pass is at the reservation headquarters, in Sacaton, forty-six miles southeast of Phoenix, by way of I-10 and Arizona 187. (520) 796-7712

SAN CARLOS

One of the largest Apache reservations in the country, San Carlos was split off from the Fort Apache grant in 1897. It is a fairly prosperous community, with investments in cattle raising and mining (its land adjoins Arizona's copper belt), as well as tourist facilities.

 Apache Gold Casino *(San Carlos Apache).* One hundred miles east of Phoenix by way of U.S. 60 and 70. (520) 425-7692.

SOMERTON

The Cocopah were an agricultural people, pushed ever south along the Colorado River Valley by the more numerous Mohave and Yuma. They were famed as steamboat pilots for pioneers crossing the river in the nineteenth century. After a period of impoverishment, they developed a farming community when the reservation was established in 1917.

 Cocopah Bingo *(Cocopah Tribe).* At 15364 S. Avenue B, about thirteen miles south of Yuma by way of U.S. 95. (602) 726-8066.

TUCSON

 Casino of the Sun *(Pascua Yaqui Tribe)*. At 7406 S. Camino de Oeste. Northern suburbs of Tucson, by way of U.S. 89. (520) 883-5092.

The Yaqui migrated into this part of Arizona from the Sonoran Desert of Mexico in the early part of the 20th Century. The hostility of the Mexican government partially motivated the move. By 1940, there were about 2,000 living around the village of Pascua, but they were not recognized as a tribe by the U.S. government and were ineligible for reservation lands. Tribal status was granted in order to open the casino.

 Desert Diamond Casino *(Tohono O'oodham Nation of the Papago)*. 7350 S. Old Nogales Highway, in the southern suburbs, by way of U.S. 89. (602) 294-7777.

Related to the agricultural Pima, the Papago were a hunting people because they had no access to water. When the San Xavier Reservation was set aside for them, in 1874, local ranchers first excluded the best grazing lands. They remain the most populous tribe in southern Arizona and their Mission San Xavier del Bac is one of the state's top attractions.

WHITERIVER

In one of the most remote parts of the state, Whiteriver is just north of the administrative headquarters of Fort Apache Reservation. Part of the oldest Apache land grant in Arizona, dating from 1871, the reservation has invested heavily in lumbering and operates a museum of Apache life, at Fort Apache.

 Hon Dah Casino *(White Mountain Apaches)*. Ninety-five miles south of I-40, by way of Arizona 77, U.S. 60 and Arizona 73. (602) 338-1560.

California

Casinos are not legal in California, with the exception of Native American casinos. For lottery information, contact the California State Lottery.

 California State Lottery 600 N. Tenth Street, Sacramento 95814. (916) 323-7095. Sales: $2.3 billion. Proceeds: $842 million. 100% Education.

ALBANY

 Golden Gate Fields, thoroughbred track. At 1100 Eastbourne Highway, from the Gilman exit of I-80; north of Berkeley. February–June. (510) 559-7300.

ALPINE

 Viejas Casino and Turf Club *(Viejas Band of Mission Indians)*. 5000 Willows Road. Twenty-five miles east of San Diego, on I-8. (619) 445-5400.

ARCADIA

 Santa Anita, one of the country's most famous thoroughbred tracks. Opened in 1934. East of downtown Los Angeles and Pasadena, at 285 W. Huntington Drive, by way of California 110 (Pasadena Freeway) and I-210 (Foothills Freeway). Wednesday-Sunday, early October–early November and December 26–late April. (818) 574-7223.

AUBERRY

The Mono lived along the western edge of the Sierra Nevada, in some of the most rugged country in California. So they held onto their lands much longer than tribes in more desirable areas. Rancherias are small tracts purchased by the U.S. government for settling Native Americans in California.

 Mono Wind Casino *(Auberry Big Sandy Rancheria)*. 37302 Rancheria Lane. Forty miles northeast of Fresno, by way of California 168. (209) 855-4350.

BIG PINE

The most numerous tribe along the eastern slope of California's Sierra, the Paiute were a hunting and gathering people who never acquired horses. When the Owens Valley was bought up for water resources by Los Angeles investors, the Paiute were moved onto several reservations.

 Sierra Spring Casino *(Big Pine Paiute Tribe of the Owens Valley)*. 545 Butcher Lane. Two-hundred fifty miles northeast of Los Angeles, on U.S. 395. (619) 938-3359.

BROOKS

 Cache Creek Bingo and Casino *(Rumsey Indian Rancheria)*. Forty-five miles northwest of Sacramento, by way of California 16. (916) 796-3118.

BURNEY

The Pit River tribe are also known as the Achomawi, a small group of tribal bands who occupied California's northern Sierra lowlands. A rancheria in this area was established for about 100 tribal members in 1938.

 Pit River Casino *(Pit River Tribe)*. 20265 Tamarack Ave. Fifty miles east of Redding on California 299. (916) 335-2334.

CABAZON

The Morongo reservation lies north of the highway and is home to descendants of the Cahuilla and Serrano tribes whose lands were taken away during the mission era.

 Casino Morongo *(Morongo Band of Mission Indians)*. 49750 Seminole Drive. Twenty miles west of Palm Springs, by way of I-10. (909) 849-3080.

COACHELLA

 Spotlight 29 Casino *(Twenty Nine Palms Band of Mission Indians)*. 46-200 Harrison Street. Thirty-five miles west of Palm Springs, by way of I-10. (619) 775-5566.

COLUSA

The history of the Wintun has been one of almost unrelieved disaster. They were the most numerous tribe in northwestern California at the start of the nineteenth century, but seventy-five percent were wiped out in an epidemic by 1833. Ranchers stole their lands, mine operations fouled their water supply and dam-construction flooded the land they retained. Less than 1,000 survive.

 Colusa Indian Bingo *(Colusa Band of Wintun Indians)*. Seventy-five miles north of Sacramento, by way of I-5. (916) 458-8844.

CRESCENT CITY

 Elk Valley Casino *(Elk Valley Rancheria)*. Eighty miles north of Eureka on U.S. 101. (707) 464-1020.

DEL MAR

 Del Mar Thoroughbred Club. At the San Diego County Fairgrounds, off I-5, fifteen miles north of downtown San Diego. Wednesday–Sunday, late July–mid-September. (619) 755-1141.

EL CAJON

This canyon country reservation is occupied by the descendants of the Kumeyaay band of Mission Indians.

 Sycuan Indian Bingo and Poker Casino. 5469 Dehesa Road. In the eastern suburbs of San Diego, along I-8. (619) 445-6002.

FRIANT

The rancheria is occupied by members of the Mono and Chickansi tribes, traditional occupants of the Sierra's western slopes near the Central Valley.

 Table Mountain Rancheria Casino and Bingo, 8184 Table Mountain Road. Twenty-one miles north of Fresno, by way of California 41 and 145. (209) 822-2485.

HAVASU

A small nomadic tribe, the Chemehuevi broke away from the Southern Paiute in the late ninteenth century and moved into Mohave lands along the Colorado. But smallpox, land grabs and flooding reduced their numbers to about 400. They did receive $900,000 in restitution for the flooding of their lands by Parker Dam.

 Havasu Landing Resort and Casino *(Chemehuevi Indian Tribe).* 1 Main Street. Across the Colorado River from Lake Havasu, Arizona, with connections by ferryboat. (619) 858-4219.

HIGHLAND

The inhabitants of this area are mostly descendants of the Serrano tribe.

 San Manuel Indian Bingo and Casino *(San Manuel Band of Mission Indians).* 5797 N. Victoria Avenue. Eastern suburbs of San Bernardino, by way of California 30. (909) 864-5050.

HOOPA

Because of their remote location along the Trinity and Klamath Rivers, the Hoopa, unlike most California tribes, still live in their ancestral homeland. The reservation was set aside for them in 1864 and it remains the largest in the state.

 Lucky Bear Casino and Bingo *(Hoopa Valley Tribe)*. Sixty miles northeast of Eureka by way of California 299 and 96. (916) 625-4048.

HOPLAND

The Pomo once occupied the Russian River Valley and were the most powerful tribal group in the area north of San Francisco. They worked at the Russian settlement in Fort Ross, but were decimated and enslaved by Spanish, Mexican and American forces. They live now on several rancherias in this area.

 Hopland Sho-ka-wah Casino *(Hopland Band of Pomo Indians)*. 13101 Nakomis Road. Ninety miles north of the Golden Gate Bridge on U.S. 101. (707) 744-1395.

INDIO

This small band of Mission Indians runs the casino amid the luxurious resorts and golf courses in the fashionable east end of the Palm Springs area.

 Cabazon Bingo and Fantasy Springs Casino *(Cabazon Band of Mission Indians)*. 84-245 B Indio Springs Drive, off California 111 in the eastern suburbs of Palm Springs. (619) 342-2593.

INGLEWOOD

 Hollywood Park. Another of the landmark tracks in southern California, with a season complementing that of Santa Anita. At 1050 S. Prairie Avenue and Century Boulevard, south of downtown, west off I-110 (Harbor Freeway). 1 p.m., Wednesday–Sunday, mid–April to late July and mid–November to late December. (310) 419-1500.

JACKSON

This band of Miwuk had the misfortune to be situated right in the midst of the Gold Rush area. Their lands lost long ago, they were settled on rancherias in the vicinity.

 Jackson Indian Bingo and Casino *(Jackson Rancheria Band of Miwuk Indians)*. 12222 New York Ranch Road. Sixty-five miles east of Sacramento by way of California 16 and 49. (209) 223-1677.

JAMESTOWN

The eastern branch of the Miwuk held land in the middle of the California gold fields. Many of them worked as miners during the Gold Rush era, but afterwards they lost most of their property. A few rancherias were set aside for them early in the twentieth century.

 Chicken Ranch Bingo *(Chicken Ranch Band of Miwuk Indians)*. Seventy miles east of Stockton, by way of California 4 and 49. (209) 984-3000.

LAKESIDE

Barona Ranch is a branch of the larger Capitan Grande Reservation of Mission Indians, located in the rugged canyonlands behind El Cajon Mountain.

 Barona Casino and Bingo *(Barona Band of Mission Indians)*. 1000 Wildcat Canyon Road. In the eastern suburbs of San Diego, by way of I-8 and California 67. (619) 443-2300.

LEMOORE

The Tachi were a branch of the Yokut people, who occupied the San Joaquin Valley in the area south of Fresno. At their peak, the Yokut may have numbered as many as 50,000. About 100 members of this band live on the rancheria.

 Palace Indian Gaming Center *(Santa Rosa Band of Tachi Indians)*. Thirty-one miles south of Fresno by way of California 41. (209) 924-7751.

LOS ALAMITOS

 Los Alamitos Race Course. The Orange County track, with thoroughbred, quarter horse and harness racing. At 4961 E. Katella Avenue, east off 1-605 (San Gabriel River Freeway). All year. (714) 995-1234.

NICE

Closely related to the group that operates the Pomo casino at Hopland.

 Robinson Racheria Bingo and Casino *(Robinson Rancheira of Pomo Indians).* 1545 E. Highway 20. Thirty-five miles east from U.S. 101 at Hopland by way of California 175, 29 and 20. (707) 275-9000.

OROVILLE

The Maidu were the most numerous Native people in the area south of Lassen Peak. They were decimated by epidemics and gold fever.

 Feather Falls Casino *(Mooretown Rancheria).* 3 Alverda Drive. Seventy-five miles north of Sacramento, by way of California 99 and 70. (916) 533-0289.

 Gold Country Casino *(Tyme Maidu Tribe of the Berry Creek Rancheria).* 4020 Olive Highway. (916) 534-9892.

PALM SPRINGS

A perfect winter climate makes Palm Springs one of America's top resort areas. It also made the Agua Caliente one of the country's wealthiest tribes. They are the primary landowners in Palm Springs and operate this casino in one of the town's most venerable hotels.

 Spa Hotel and Casino *(Agua Caliente Band of Cahuilla Indians).* 140 N. Indian Canyon Drive, downtown Palm Springs. (619) 323-5865.

PLEASANTON

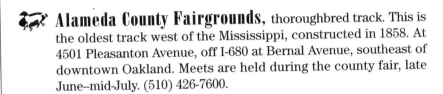 **Alameda County Fairgrounds,** thoroughbred track. This is the oldest track west of the Mississippi, constructed in 1858. At 4501 Pleasanton Avenue, off I-680 at Bernal Avenue, southeast of downtown Oakland. Meets are held during the county fair, late June–mid-July. (510) 426-7600.

REDDING

 **Win-River Casino Bingo** *(Redding Rancheria).* 2100 Redding Rancheria Road. (916) 243-3377.

SAN JACINTO

Soboba Legends Casino *(Soboba Band of Mission Indians).* Forty miles southeast of San Bernardino, by way of 1-10 and California 79.(909) 654-2883.

SAN MATEO

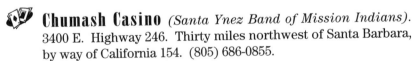 **Bay Meadows,** thoroughbred track. California 92 at Hillsdale Boulevard, south of San Francisco on U.S. 101. Opens at 1 p.m., Wednesday–Sunday, late August–late January. (415) 574-7223.

SANTA YNEZ

About fifty descendants of the Chumash, who occupied the coastal area around Santa Barbara, now live on this small reserve. They were one of the first tribal groups to be almost totally converted to mission status.

Chumash Casino *(Santa Ynez Band of Mission Indians).* 3400 E. Highway 246. Thirty miles northwest of Santa Barbara, by way of California 154. (805) 686-0855.

SUSANVILLE

Northern Lights Casino *(Susanville Indian Rancheria).* 900 Skyline Drive. Eighty-five miles northwest of Reno, Nevada, by way of U.S. 395. (916) 252-1102.

TEMECULA

Remnants of the Luiseno people, transferred to the missions by Spain in the late eighteenth century, live here. Their ancestral homes were along the coast, north of San Diego.

 Pechanga Entertainment Center *(Temecula Band of Luiseno Mission Indians)*. 45000 Pala Road. Sixty miles north of San Diego on I-15. (909) 693-1819.

TRINIDAD

The inhabitants of the rancheria are Yurok, who lived on the northern California coastline and were associated with the Hoopa.

 Cher-Ae Heights Bingo and Casino *(Trinidad Rancheria)*. Twenty-two miles north of Eureka on U.S. 101. (707) 677-3611.

WINTERHAVEN

The Quechan are a branch of the Yuma tribe, which occupied both sides of the Colorado near its junction with the Gila River. The Fort Yuma Reservation was established for them in 1883, but the remaining 9,000 acres of Quechan land is now on the California side. A tribal museum sits on a hill overlooking Yuma and the historic river crossing.

 Paradise Casino *(Quechan Indian Tribe)*. 350 Picacho Road. Across the Colorado River from Yuma, Arizona. (619) 572-0213.

Colorado

When casino gambling returned to Colorado, it was limited to three towns. All three have historical roots connected to the biggest gamble of all—gold mining. Black Hawk, Central City and Cripple Creek rose out of Colorado's canyons and hills as mining camps, then declined into almost-deserted hamlets. Although they were not quite ghost towns, they were fairly much on economic life support systems. Casinos have brought back much of an Old West flavor to places in which they were an authentic part of historic reality.

Games permitted under Colorado gaming laws are blackjack, slots, video poker and video keno. For lottery information contact the Colorado State Lottery.

 Colorado State Lottery: 201 W. Eighth Street, Suite 600, Denver 81003. (719) 546-2400. Sales: $331 million. Proceeds: $91 million. 36% Conservation Trust Fund; 34% capital construction; 21% environmental and wildlife programs; 9% state parks.

AURORA

 Arapaho Park, thoroughbred track. At 26000 E. Quincy, off U.S. 40, east of downtown Denver. Daily, May–September. (303) 690-2400.

BLACK HAWK

On May 6, 1859, John H. Gregory struck gold in a gulch that would soon bear his name. The first major lode discovered in Colorado, it transformed the entire territory within a matter of months. The sparsely-populated mountains suddenly became a magnet for hordes of treasure seekers racing westward across Kansas or back east from the California diggings. "Pikes Peak or Bust" became the cry of the nation as the wealth of these canyons began to flow. In just seventeen years, Colorado became a state, far earlier than any of its neighbors in the Rockies. Most historians credit that to the gold of Gregory Gulch.

A bit of subterfuge was employed to spark initial interest in the gulch. New York newspaper editor Horace Greeley, always a Western booster, showed up to investigate the stories of Colorado gold. Some local fun-lovers "salted" one of the streams, placing gold dust where it would easily be found. Greeley's enthusiastic reports helped feed the gold frenzy.

Black Hawk, which adjoins Central City on the east, grew up as a smelting center and foundry for mining machinery. But there were significant gold strikes made there, too. All told, an estimated $67 million in gold was taken from Gregory Gulch over its history. Black Hawk is located thirty miles west of Denver, by way of I-70 and Colorado 119. Nineteen casinos, open daily from 8 a.m. to 2 a.m.

Bronco Billy's II, at 125 Gregory Street. (303) 582-3311.

Bullwhackers, at 101 Gregory Street. (303) 271-2072.

Crooks Palace, at 200 Gregory Street. (303) 582-5094.

El Dorado Casino, at 131 Gregory Street. (800) 271-0711.

Gilpin Hotel Casino, at 111 Main Street. (303) 582-1133.

Gold Mine Casino, at 130 Clear Creek. (303) 428-0711.

Golden Canary, at 231 Gregory Street. (303) 582-1701.

Golden Gates Casino, at 261 Main Street. (303) 582-1650.

Jazz Alley Casino, at 320 Main Street. (303) 582-1125.

Lilly Belle's, at 301 Gregory Street. (303) 582-5000.

Otto's Casino, at 260 Gregory Street. (303) 642-0415.

Pick-a-Dilly Casino, at 121 Main Street. (303) 582-1844.

CENTRAL CITY

Central City got its name because of its location, about midway down the gulch in the center of the mining camps. It quickly became

The Teller House

The Teller House, the grand hotel dating from 1872, was built by Henry M. Teller, who rode the fortune he made here to national political power. At its opening, it was billed as the finest hotel between St. Louis and San Francisco. The high point of its early years was the visit paid by President Grant in 1873, when a path of silver bricks was laid down for his benefit from the road to the front door. The old hostelry now contains one of the town's casinos and a version of the fabled "Face on the Barroom Floor," as well. Some pop culture historians insist the original poem, about a vagabond artist drawing the face of the woman who drove him mad, referred to a chalk painting in a saloon in Ohio. But Central City residents claim this is the real deal and say it has been a part of the Teller House since the 1890s.

the biggest. It was three times the size of Denver, described as "the richest square mile on Earth" and seriously considered for the state capital. It was noted for its orderly miners' courts and some of the state's most powerful political leaders, including its first two U.S. Senators. One of the first Senators from Montana and George Pullman, who would make a fortune with his railroad sleeping car, came from Central City. The Opera House, opened in 1878, was a landmark of the West and the greatest names in theater and music performed there. But in just ten more years, the mines were played out, the crowds left and the long silence returned to Gregory Gulch.

It was the old opera house that carried the seeds of the town's revival. Starting in 1932, summer theater and music festivals were held here, with Lillian Gish starring in *Camille* as the first attraction. It became a summer tradition for residents of Denver and tourists from around the country to make the trip to the tumbledown old town and take in a performance. After World War II, investors began restoring its main street to the look of the 1870s and Central City was turned into a tourist attraction.

Central City adjoins Black Hawk on the west. There are twelve casinos concentrated on Main and Lawrence Streets, open daily from 8 a.m. to 2 a.m.

 Baby Doe's Silver Dollar Casino, at 102A Lawrence Street. (303) 582-5510.

 Bullwhacker's, at 130 Main Street. (303) 271-2600.

🎲 **Central Palace Casino,** at 132 Lawrence Street. (303) 582-0637.

🎲 **Dillon's Double Eagle,** at 161 Lawrence Street. (303) 582-3257.

🎲 **Golden Rose Casino,** at 120 Main Street. (303) 582-5060.

🎲 **Harrah's Casino,** at 131 Main Street. (303) 777-1111.

🎲 **Harvey's Wagon Wheel Casino,** at 321 Gregory Street. (303) 582-0800.

🎲 **Long Branch Saloon and Casino,** at 123 Main Street. (303) 582-0704.

🎲 **Silver Slipper,** at 98-100 Lawrence Street. (303) 582-0100.

🎲 **Teller House,** at 120 Eureka Street. (303) 279-3200.

🎲 **Toll Gate Casino,** at 108 Main Street. (303) 582-5424.

CRIPPLE CREEK

Just as the gold petered out at Gregory Gulch, an even bigger strike came in several miles to the south. The Cripple Creek area had been thoroughly combed over during the Pike's Peak rush of the late 1850s, but there were always rumors that a major vein had been overlooked. Individual prospectors would come out of the canyons around Mt. Pisgah with wild stories of a big strike waiting to be found. Most people passed them off as myths because there had been so many false leads and cases of outright fraud in the history of Colorado mining. Besides, by 1891 mining experts felt that most of the important veins were already known. A young cowboy, Robert Womack, believed the stories. He sank several shafts in an area called Poverty Gulch. Womack took a sample from one of them, which he had named the El Paso mine, into Colorado Springs to be assayed. When it came through at $250 a ton, he sold his claim for $500, went on a drunk and vanished from history. The rush to Cripple Creek was on.

Within five years, a city of 25,000 formed near Womack's strike. By 1901, the population was close to 50,000 and more gold than any other place in the United States was being taken out of here, close to $25 million in that year alone. What made the finds especially valuable was that they coincided with the crash of the price for silver in 1893.

While the great strikes at Leadville and Aspen were closing down, the gold of Cripple Creek was reaching its crest.

At its peak, there were eleven different camps in the area, which was named for a rocky stream that injured the feet of cattle trying to cross it. After fire wiped out most of the first settlement in 1906, the town was rebuilt on modern lines, with cement sidewalks, brick buildings and a system of electric railways. Future heavyweight champions Jack Johnson and Jack Dempsey (who was born in another Colorado mining camp) were employed here as bouncers at different times. The legendary bar owner Texas Guinan, who would go on to teach New York how to party in the 1920s, started her career here, too.

The mines started playing out after 1914. Aside from a brief resurgence of activity in the 1930s, Cripple Creek's day was over. The town never entirely died, however. Although it could be reached only by unpaved mountain roads for many years, it turned into a tourist attraction and many of the old buildings were restored. The Phantom Canyon Road, which leads here from the south, is still one of the great driving adventures in the West.

Cripple Creek is forty-one miles west of Colorado Springs, by way of US 24 and Colorado 67. Casinos are open daily, 8 a.m. to 2 a.m. The casino district runs along East Bennett Street. Most of the casinos are rather small scale, with fewer than 300 slots and four blackjack tables.

Bobby Womack's Gaming Parlor, at 210 E. Bennett Avenue (719) 689-0333.

Bronco Billy's, at 418 E. Bennett Avenue. (719) 689-2142.

Diamond Lil's, at 208 E. Bennett Avenue. (719) 689-2282.

Gold Digger's Casino, at 217 E. Bennett Avenue. (719) 689-3911.

Gold Rush Hotel and Casino, at 209 E. Bennett Avenue. (719) 689-2646.

Imperial Hotel and Casino, at 123 N. Third. (719) 689-7777.

Legends (formerly the Long Branch), at 200 E. Bennett Avenue. (719) 689-3242.

Midnight Rose Hotel and Casino, at 252 E. Bennett Avenue. (719) 689-0303.

Underground Mine Tours

One of the mines in Cripple Creek, the Mollie Kathleen, at the north edge of town, can be visited on an underground tour. The old assay office is now a museum and the narrow gauge railroad that ran to the nearby town of Victor also operates during the summer months.

CORTEZ

These reservation lands are occupied by the Weminuche band of Utes, who split off from other members of the southern branch of the tribe after 1877. The territory in Colorado's southwestern corner is rich in oil and gas, and the Utes also pursue interests in stock-raising and tourism.

 Ute Mountain Casino *(Ute Mountain Tribe).* South of town on U.S. 160, 666. (970) 565-8800.

IGNACIO

The Southern Utes live on treaty lands granted to them in 1873. More extensive territory along the entire western slope of the Rockies was withdrawn after silver was found there. They are closely related to the neighboring Ute Mountain Tribe.

 Sky Ute Casino and Lodge *(Southern Ute Indian Tribe).* 14826 Highway 172 N., twenty-four miles southeast of Durango. (970) 563-3000.

Idaho

In Idaho, gambling is available at Native American casinos and thoroughbred and harness racing tracks. For state lottery information, contact the Idaho State Lottery.

 Idaho State Lottery, 1199 Shoreline Lane, Suite 100, Boise 83707, (208)334-2600. Sales: $92 million. Proceeds: $20 million. 50% Permanent building fund; 50% Public schools.

BOISE

 Les Bois Park, thoroughbred track. At the Western Idaho Fairgrounds, west from downtown on U.S. 20, 26, then north, at 5610 Glenwood Road. Early May–August. (208)376-3991.

BONNER'S FERRY

The Kootenai were a nomadic and trading people, who lived in the Idaho panhandle and neighboring areas of Washington and British Columbia. They allied with the U.S. against their traditional Blackfoot enemies, but disease depleted their numbers to a few hundred when this reservation was established in 1895.

 Kootenai River Plaza *(Kootenai Tribe).* One hundred ten miles northeast of Spokane, Washington, by way of U.S. 2. (208)267-8511.

IDAHO FALLS

 Teton Racing, harness racing. June–August. (208)529-8722.

FORT HALL

These two tribes were allies in the mid-nineteenth century, brought together by ancestral ties and common fear of the Blackfoot. Their territory along the Snake River was the main route of the Oregon Trail and prime grazing lands were wiped out by the large number of wagon trains. Smallpox also afflicted the tribes. They fought to protect their lands but were forced to sign a treaty that placed them on the Fort Hall Reservation in 1868. A Native American gathering here in August is the largest in the Northwest.

 Shoban Exit 80 Casino *(Shoshone-Bannock Tribes)*. Fifteen miles north of Pocatello, on I-15. (208)237-8729.

LAPWAI

The Nez Perce were the most populous tribe in northern Idaho and eastern Oregon when white settlers arrived in the mid-nineteenth century. This is a portion of a much larger reservation established for them in 1855. But land grabs by miners and settlers led to the famous 1877 uprising of Chief Joseph, whose band refused to move to this shrunken tract. Instead, they fought the U.S. Army in a running 1,200-mile campaign that ended near the Canadian border in Montana. His followers were scattered to other tribal lands.

 Clearwater River Casino, *(Nez Perce Tribe)*. Ten miles east of Lewiston, on U.S. 95. (208)843-7317.

POCATELLO

 Pocatello Park at the Bannock County Fairgrounds, thoroughbred track. Off I-15 at exit 71, north of downtown. May–June and September. (208)237-1340.

WORLEY

This tribe, which moved into the area from coastal British Columbia in prehistoric times, dominated northern Idaho and the Spokane area when Europeans arrived. Resistance was crushed by the Army in 1858. A gold rush forced them to cede most of their holdings and they were restricted to this reservation after 1889.

 Coeur d'Alene Tribal Bingo. U.S. 95, thirty miles south of Coeur d'Alene. (208)523-2464.

Montana

Casino gaming in Montana is available at casinos owned by Native Americans. For lottery information, contact the Montana State Lottery.

 Montana State Lottery, 2525 N. Montana, Helena 56901, (406)444-5825. Sales: $32 million. Proceeds: $7.8 million. 100% General Fund.

BOX ELDER

The Cree were the most powerful of the Plains tribes in Canada, dominating the area between western Ontario and the Rockies. But they were defeated in repeated wars with the Blackfoot and many of them drifted south into Montana. They returned to Canada to take part in the ill-advised Riel Rebellion of 1885, an uprising of Indians and French-speaking settlers in the West against the federal government. Afterwards, some of the Cree and Chippewa participants returned to live together on this reservation, named for a Cree-Chippewa chief. This represents the westernmost advance of the Chippewa and the southernmost tract belonging to the Cree.

 4 C's Casino, *(Chippewa Cree Tribe of the Rocky Boy's Reservation).* Rocky Boy Road, ninety-five miles northeast of Great Falls, on U.S. 87. (406)395-4863.

BROWNING

The Blackfoot people were accomplished hunters, ranging across the Northern Plains in what is now Montana and Alberta. Frequently at war with their neighbors, their way of life ended with the disappearance of the buffalo herds. Forced onto reservations in both Canada and the United States, they suffered from drought in the 1880s when they attempted to become agricultural. Since then, they have been successful as stockmen and also developed a tourist trade on the access highway to Glacier National Park, including an excellent museum in Browning.

 Blackfeet Bingo, *(Blackfeet Tribe).* Thirty-one miles southest of the eastern entrance to Glacier National Park, on U.S. 89. (406)338-5751.

CROW AGENCY

Located along the Little Big Horn River and with a freeway running through it, the Crow Reservation is the site of the Custer Battlefield and does much tourist business. The Crows also developed ranching interests on their land, which is near their ancestral territory. The Crow generally allied themselves with U.S. forces in the nineteenth century wars with the Dakota, and while their reservations lands were sliced, they fared better than most other Plains tribes.

 Absaloka Casino, *(Crow Indian Tribe).* Sixty miles east of Billings on I-90. (406)638-4444.

GREAT FALLS

 State Fair, thoroughbred track. Off I-15 Business, across the Missouri River bridge from downtown. June–August. (406)727-8900.

LAME DEER

The Cheyenne tribe split into northern and southern branches in 1832, with the southern half moving to the area of Bent's trading post in Colorado. The northern portion remained in Montana and allied themselves with the Dakota to resist the spread of settlement. This campaign climaxed in the nearby Battle of the Little Big Horn in 1876. Afterwards, the northern tribe was removed to Oklahoma to join their brethren. A group escaped in 1878 and tried to fight their way back home in a running battle against the U.S. Cavalry. Finally captured and taken back south, the Cheyenne were permitted to return legally when this reservation was established for them in 1884.

Northern Cheyenne Social Club, *(Northern Cheyenne Tribe)*. One-hundred-three miles east of Billings by way of I-90 and U.S. 212. (406)477-6677.

WOLF POINT

The Assiniboine and Sioux are linguistically related and may have lived in proximity to each other along the Minnesota-Ontario border in the eighteenth century. The Assiniboine then broke away and headed west across Canada, living around Lake Winnipeg and becoming deeply involved with the fur trade and Hudson's Bay Co. Their numbers reduced by war and disease, they moved onto reservations on both sides of the international border in the 1880s and were joined at Fort Peck by western branches of the Sioux.

 Silverwolf Casino, *(Assiniboine and Sioux Tribes of the Fort Peck Reservation)*. Highway 13 West, ninety-five miles west of Williston, North Dakota, on U.S. 2. (406)653-3476.

Nevada

For almost a century it was the Empty Quarter on the map of America. It was a vast, lonely space; the barrier before reaching the formidable Sierra Nevada and the final leg to the golden riches of California. Spanish explorers first entered the state's southern area, searching for a trail from Santa Fe to California, in the late seventeenth century. They never found it, but they brought reports of a river that penetrated the mountains and flowed into the Pacific. Those stories persisted for decades, luring trappers and adventurers into the wilderness of Nevada in a search for this nonexistent stream.

Mormons came in from their Utah settlements and tried to farm the thin band of fertile land that lay on the eastern slope of the Sierra, but Brigham Young called them back after a few years. Other explorers tracked the Humboldt River. Its valley through northern Nevada became the main route from the Oregon Trail to the gold rush towns of California. No one gave a thought or a name to Nevada. It was just the desert travelers went through to get to where they really wanted to go.

Nonetheless, a hearty band of settlers, including many living in what is now California, petitioned Congress for recognition as a territory in the late 1850s. Congress counted noses and waved off the request. They were tens of thousands below the minimum population required for territorial status. Then two things happened: the Comstock Lode came in and the Civil War began.

The Comstock, discovered in 1859, was the biggest silver strike in American history. It turned barren Nevada into a boom area as thousands of busted California miners recrossed the mountains to try their luck in this new bonanza. A significant number were Southerners, which worried the federal authorities. War was approaching and Washington wanted to keep this treasure trove securely in the Union. In a sudden policy reversal, a territorial act was rushed through Congress and signed by President James Buchanan in early 1861. Within three years Nevada had become a state.

But like every other state with an economic base of mining, Nevada was susceptible to huge, unpredictable cycles of boom and bust. When the Comstock played out in the early 1880s, it appeared that Nevada's statehood was a joke. Within twenty years, it had lost one-third of its population. By 1900, just a little more than 40,000 people remained in its vacant expanse. That's when the second big strike came in, the silver and gold of Tonopah and Goldfield. But that, too, played itself out, and by the late 1920s, Nevada again seemed to be a place without a future.

Then three extraordinary events changed the course of its history forever. The Boulder Dam project was approved in 1928, touching off a construction and water boom that would transform the southern part of the state, centered around Las Vegas. The state's economy soared to its highest levels since the Comstock days. Then in the spring of 1931 the state legislature passed two astonishing measures. The first reduced the waiting time for a divorce to six weeks and the second legalized gambling. A lot of illegal gambling was going on behind closed doors, anyhow. Nevadans felt it was part of the state's free-wheeling tradition and saw nothing wrong with it. Why not, they reasoned, make a little money from it, too. They had no idea how much would come in.

The boom hit Reno first. Already the state's largest community, ("The biggest little city in the world" became its boast) Reno soon exploded with facilities for tourists, gamblers and women establishing residency for a quickie divorce. The term "Renovate," coined by columnist Walter Winchell to describe celebrity Nevada divorces, entered the language.

The larger explosion was waiting to happen. Las Vegas had developed as a watering place for livestock along a branch of the Old Spanish Trail. It had barely 10,000 people when work began on nearby Boulder Dam. The massive project turned the town into a recreational center. The state gambling act specifically excluded Boulder City, construction headquarters for the dam. The federal government did not like the idea of its employees blowing their paychecks in such an unseemly manner. Boulder City remains the largest town in the state to exclude gambling. But that meant Las Vegas, less than an hour away over fast desert road, would get all the business. A downtown casino area was in full operation by the end of the 1930s.

It remained for the visionary mobster, Benjamin ("Bugsy") Siegel, to see the larger possibilities. Las Vegas already had become a weekend destination for affluent residents of Los Angeles. The available accommodations were fairly ordinary, however. They tended to be simple and basic Old West in tone rather than Hollywood luxurious. Siegel set about to change all that. Supported by mob money, he built the Flamingo Hotel in 1947. Sparing no expense, he erected a vision of excess that would become the standard for an incredible fantasy world that would rise on the desert floor.

Unfortunately for Siegel, much of the money was not his to spend. When his resort got off to a slow start he paid for the over-indulgence with his life. Within a few years, however, his vision was realized. One gigantic hotel after another, each more ornate and fantastic than the last, opened on a desert road that was transformed into The Strip. It became the center of America's entertainment industry, where gambling profits supported an incredible array of showrooms, lavish revues, inexpensive meals, free drinks. With mob money pouring into the place, virtually every human vice could be satisfied. It called itself a "Disneyland for Adults," and the phrase Las Vegas Showgirl came to symbolize the epitome of statuesque and available beauty.

In the 1970s, however, Las Vegas faced the first serious threat to its dominance. Gambling was legalized in Atlantic City. All at once, the big money out of the East Coast had another place to go. But one perceptive casino owner saw an alternative way. Bill Bennett opened Circus Circus as a small operation in 1968 and expanded it steadily over the next eighteen years. It was, of all things, a family-oriented resort hotel. Rooms were priced at next to nothing and circus acts, instead of bare-breasted chorines, played all day to an enthusiastic audience of kids. The rest of Las Vegas thought Bennett had gone bonkers. But by the 1980s, his concept had transformed the entire city. Las Vegas had become a family place.

Not only that, it was the fastest growing urban area in America. People came first to frolic and then returned to settle in because of the mild desert climate and endless options for entertainment. Former Californians, fed up with rising taxes, unaffordable housing and crime, flocked across the border to retire or start life again. Businesses followed and Nevada's economy diversified as never before.

By the 1990s, Las Vegas had become one of the world's top travel destinations. The first generation of showplace hotels had been leveled and replaced by even more spectacular structures. Most of them were themed, virtual indoor amusement parks. There were more hotel rooms at a single intersection on The Strip than in most American cities. The proliferation of legalized gaming across the country only seemed to make Las Vegas more prosperous. Instead of competition, the new casinos whetted the appetites of customers for the real thing, the genuine Las Vegas experience. By 1990, there were 750,000 people living in the metropolitan area, more than were in the entire state in 1970.

U.S. 50, which runs across the center of the state, is still described as "the loneliest road in America." Ruins of Pony Express stables can be found just a few hundred yards off the concrete pavement. The old emptiness awaits only a few miles off any major highway. But the state that gambling built is no longer America's empty quarter. The bet it had made on legalization in 1931 turned out to be the biggest winner in American history.

Almost every community in the state has casino gambling in some form. There are, however, six major concentrations in Nevada: Carson City, Henderson, Lake Tahoe, Las Vegas, Laughlin and Reno-Sparks.

CARSON CITY

This place long ago shed its tag as the smallest capital in the United States. Carson City is now a thriving community of 40,000 souls. However, along with Baton Rouge, Louisiana, it is the only seat of government in the country that permits casino gambling within its limits.

Named for the legendary scout Kit Carson, the place grew up at the first green space after the long trek across the bleak Nevada wilderness. Some weary settlers who had come this far saw no reason to test the hazards of the Sierras. They became Carson City's first residents. Their numbers multiplied when disappointed returnees from the California gold fields began moving in during the 1850s. After the brief Mormon settlement in nearby Genoa, Nevada's first town, was discontinued, Carson City managed to get the territorial capital moved here. Correspondingly, the main route of the Pony Express and transcontinental telegraph came through the place, along the overland stage trail now followed by U.S. 50.

Most of the city's casinos are clustered along Carson Street, (U.S. 395), the city's main north-south throughfare. All are open daily, twenty-four hours. Most are on the smallish side, offering about a dozen blackjack tables, 300 slots and one or two craps tables. The $2 minimum bet is fairly standard.

Cactus Jack's Casino, 420 N. Carson Street, (702) 882-8770. The town's only poker room and an innovative collection of slots are the big attractions here. There are 210 machines, three blackjack tables and two poker tables.

Carson Horseshoe, at 402 N. Carson Street (702) 883-2211. Slots and video poker only.

Carson Nugget, 507 N. Carson Street, (702) 882-1626. Not only the biggest casino in town, but it is billed as something of a museum, too. Its displays of gold, including nuggets that came out of Nevada's historic diggings, act as an inspiration for visitors. In addition to a large selection of restaurants, the Carson Nugget adjoins a motor inn.

Museums in Carson City

Carson's capitol building, with its distinctive silver dome, was completed in 1871. While it is no longer the formal seat of government, the structure is maintained as a museum. A U.S. mint was built here to coin the silver coming out of the Comstock Lode, and it operated until 1893. It is now the State Museum and displays various aspects of Nevada's history, including a mine replica and a ghost town.

 Carson Station, at 900 S. Carson Street (702) 883-0900. Seven blackjack tables, 250 slots, sports book, one craps table. Hotel attached.

 Ormsby House, 600 S. Carson Street (702) 882-1890. This is the capital's best-known hotel name. The original was built in the 1860s and was a hangout for politicians during the early days of statehood. It was named for Major William Ormsby, a local political leader killed in a raid on Paiute settlements in 1860. The kidnaping of several Indian women had sparked tribal resentment and Ormsby's force, sent to punish the Paiute, was instead almost wiped out at Pyramid Lake. The contemporary version of the famed old hotel retains an Old West atmosphere and is locally famous for its Basque cooking, especially lamb dishes. The casino features twelve blackjack tables, 385 slots, and single tables for poker, roulette and pai-gow poker.

HENDERSON

This is one of the few communities that grew up after gambling came to Nevada in which the activity was an afterthought. Henderson was built as a company town around a magnesium plant during World War II. It is now the state's industrial center, with large chemical installations, and Nevada's third biggest city. Gambling came here as a convenience since it is not permitted in Boulder City, the next town down the road. Henderson is also noted for its locally famous chocolate factory, Ethel M, which offers self-guided tours.

The town's twenty casinos are located along the Boulder Highway (U.S. 93) and are, for the most part, small establishments, catering to a local clientele. Henderson is thirteen miles south of Las Vegas. Casinos are open daily, twenty-four hours.

181

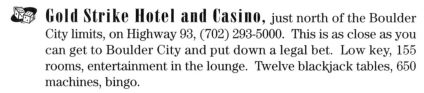

Gold Strike Hotel and Casino, just north of the Boulder City limits, on Highway 93, (702) 293-5000. This is as close as you can get to Boulder City and put down a legal bet. Low key, 155 rooms, entertainment in the lounge. Twelve blackjack tables, 650 machines, bingo.

Nevada Palace Hotel and Casino, at 5255 Boulder Highway, (702) 458-8810. An understated and pleasant facility, with family-oriented, affordable restaurants. Ten blackjack tables, 650 machines, sports book with four screens, bingo.

Railroad Pass Hotel and Casino, at 2800 S. Boulder Highway, (702) 294-5000. Good assortment of Native American pottery, large dinner buffet, excellent views of the desert from its bar. 120 rooms in the adjoining motor inn. Ten blackjack tables, 640 slots, bingo.

JACKPOT

The name says it all. Flush against the Idaho border on U.S. 93, the stopover is meant to attract gamblers from that state. This road was the main southern cutoff from the Oregon Trail to California, by way of the Humboldt Valley. The town is fifty miles south of Twin Falls, Idaho and sixty-eight miles north of I-80 from the Wells exit.

Cactus Pete's Resort Hotel and Casino, (702) 755-2321. A ten-story high, 293-room hotel, featuring a heated outdoor pool, tennis courts and golf. Two restaurants, buffet, lounge.

Horseshu Hotel and Casino, (702) 755-7777. A motel containing 120 rooms within a three-story building. Golf course, outdoor heated pool. No restaurant.

JEAN

Built for travelers from Los Angeles on I-15 who simply cannot wait to make it all the way to Las Vegas. This is the first casino concentration across the Nevada line. The town originated as a whistle stop on the Union Pacific and while its permanent population has not grown much, its transient residents now number in the thousands. The town is thirty-one miles south of downtown Las Vegas.

Primadonna Resort and Casino, (702) 382-1212. Built by one of the large Vegas casino operators, the Primadonna is a 660-room hotel. It has a conference center, golf course, bowling

Gambling with History

For a unique gaming experience, visit one of the state's old mining towns. Nevada is littered with them. Some of the most atmospheric are:

• **Eureka.** A silver boomtown from 1870 to 1891, with quite a lot of lead mined here, as well. Most of the buildings still standing here date from those years and they add up to a museum of Victorian architecture on the frontier. Eureka is about halfway across the state on U.S. 50. It is not near anyplace else and that is the appeal. Alpine Lodge and Nevada Casino, (702) 237-5365.

• **Tonopah.** Its silver rush came along a few years after Eureka's. Prospector Jim Butler found the vein in 1900 and was too broke to have it assayed. He borrowed the necessary funds and when the results came in the assayer quit his job to join the rush. It was one of Nevada's largest cities in the first decade of the twentieth century. That was when the historic Mizpah Hotel was built. Mizpah was also the name of Butler's mine, a Biblical reference to a watchtower. The old hotel houses the town's largest casino. (702) 482-6202. Tonopah is on U.S. 95, about midway between Reno and Las Vegas.

• **Virginia City.** This was the home of the Comstock Lode, celebrated by Mark Twain and one of the most famous mining camps in the Old West. The silver strike here was responsible for making Nevada a state. Today, Virginia City is one of the best preserved former camps in the country, a museum city. It features several small casinos in vintage structures along C Street.

alley, and a small amusement center for children. Two restaurants and buffet.

 Whiskey Pete's Hotel and Casino, (702) 382-4388. 777 rooms in a nineteen-story tower. Pool, water sports area with boat rentals, golf. Three restaurants, buffet.

LAKE TAHOE

The first European to see this magnificent mountain lake was probably John Fremont. During his exploration of 1844 along the valley of the Truckee, Indians told him about a big lake which was the source of the river. He followed their directions, crossed what is now Carson

Pass and found himself gazing down on a blue expanse surrounded by the snow-capped heights of the Sierra.

Tahoe was created by a massive slippage of earth during the upthrust that formed the mountains, although Native American legends speak of a barrier put down by the Great Spirit to assist a man trying to elude evil demons. Visitors are always impressed by the clarity of its water and the unique blue-green color that gives it an air of shimmering brilliance.

The lake had long been a favorite gathering place for nearby tribes, who fished its waters and also used it for water-based competitions. Fremont called it Lake Bonpland, after a French explorer, but that never caught on. Instead, eighteen years after Fremont arrived, it was officially named Tahoe in the first published map of the area. It is a Washoe word meaning lake, and the head of the mapping committee liked the sound of it. As beautiful as it was, the place was nearly desolated when surrounding timberlands were indiscriminately harvested to provide wood for supports in the tunnels of the Comstock Lode mines. Only the depletion of the silver strike saved Tahoe's natural beauty.

By 1900 it had become a summer resort for the wealthy and the first casinos opened in the 1940s. While population pressure is a constant threat to its health, the lake is protected by both federal regulations and a regional planning agency. The agency is composed of representatives from California and Nevada, since it straddles the border between the states. Gambling is permitted only on the Nevada side.

One cluster of resorts is situated on the lake's north shore and another on the south. Lake cruises and scenic drives are available on either shore. The main advantage of the north shore is that is more easily accessible from I-80, the main highway between Reno and San Francisco. It is also more secluded than the south shore, which features a strip-like ambience at the resort of Stateline.

LAKE TAHOE: THE NORTH SHORE

Incline Village is forty-six miles southwest of Reno, by way of U.S. 395, 50 and Nevada 28. Nevada 431 cuts about thirteen miles off the trip but it is mountainous and not recommended in bad weather. Crystal Bay is fifty miles southwest of Reno, by way of I-80, California 267 and Nevada 28.

Cal-Neva Lodge, Stateline Road, in Crystal Bay, (702) 832-4000. The state line runs right down the center of this property, which was the first major casino established on the north shore of Tahoe. In the months after gambling was legalized but Prohibition was still the law, the ban on booze was largely ignored here and the Cal-Neva became famous as a place where celebrities and gangsters met to drink and bet. It also developed as a favorite wedding chapel for celebrities. Frank Sinatra once owned an interest and local historians will tell you that the careers of Spike Jones and Pearl Bailey began in its showroom, which still features big name entertainment. The casino is about half the size of the Hyatt, but its poker room is highly regarded.

 Crystal Bay Club, in Crystal Bay, (702) 831-0512. Ten black-jack tables ($2 minimum), 100 machines, one craps table.

 Hyatt Regency Lake Tahoe Resort and Casino, Country Club Drive at the lakeshore, off Nevada 28, at Incline Village, (702) 831-1111. This is the pre-eminent luxury hotel and casino on this shore, with immaculately kept grounds gently descending to the water in a setting of pines and mountains. The atmosphere is more like a country club, with full recreational facilities, than other resorts on the Nevada side. Twenty-three blackjack tables ($3 minimum), 411 slots, three craps tables. There are also poker tables and a sport book here, as well as big name entertainment.

 Tahoe Biltmore Lodge, in Crystal Bay, (702) 831-0660. Hotel attached. Ten blackjack tables ($2 minimim), video poker, pai gow poker, one craps table.

LAKE TAHOE: THE SOUTH SHORE

The Casino Center is located along U.S. 50, in the town of State-line, forty-nine miles south of Reno, by way of U.S. 395 and 50.

 Caesar's Tahoe, (702) 588-3515. A northern branch of the famed Las Vegas facility. Full recreational facilities, lake views, arcade with exclusive shops, imaginatively designed pool area. Showroom with big name entertainment, including cabaret and outdoor sports arena. The casino itself is 40,000 square feet, with 45 blackjack tables, more than 1,000 slots, poker room and sports book with twelve big-screen televisions.

 Harrah's Lake Tahoe Resort and Casino, (702) 588-6606. Noted for its large hotel rooms, most of which are angled for the best lake view. Excellent health club and shopping arcade. Big name entertainment. The casino is approximately twice as large as Caesar's with ninety-eight blackjack tables and almost 2,000 slots, as well as bingo and baccarat rooms.

 Harvey's Resort Hotel and Casino, (702) 588-2411. The first and biggest of the south shore resorts with 740 rooms. It is located right at the lakeshore for unencumbered views over the water. Guests also receive free breakfasts. Health club, shopping, top entertainment. Harvey's has accumulated more than 2,000 slots, the biggest in the area. Its casino is mid-sized and regarded as being a bit friendlier towards the novice gambler.

 Horizon Casino Resort, (702) 588-6211. A smaller alternative to the three mega-resorts listed above on the south shore. There are 520 hotel rooms, a showroom, and three hot tubs outdoors. The Horizon Casino is smaller and emphasizes lower betting limits.

LAS VEGAS

If the West is the book of American legend, Las Vegas is an entire chapter in itself. It is the ultimate twentieth century boomtown; born of dreams, growing up in excess and finally settling down to a happy family life. It is American popular culture magnified and glorified. Avarice and entertainment wrapped up in one glitzy package. Liberal slots and gargantuan buffets, hotels that are more like theme parks, lots of bread and Circus Circuses, wedding chapels and Elvis impersonators and the Liberace museum, the Rat Pack and the Sultan of Insults, heavyweight championship bouts and lightweight lounge acts. Love it or hate it, there is absolutely nothing else like it on the planet.

It's been quite a ride for a place that started out, literally, as a hole in the ground. The name means "The Meadows." Travelers on the long desert crossing knew they could get fresh water from natural springs that emerged here from the earth. It became a campground on the Old Spanish Trail from Santa Fe to Los Angeles. Explorer John Fremont visited it and a Mormon colony was sent out from Salt Lake City to attempt a permanent settlement in 1855. That lasted only two years. Then The Meadows became a military outpost as Union soldiers were sent to guard the strategic springs during the Civil War. Afterwards, various settlers and miners resided in the area but no real town developed.

That ended on May 15, 1905. Promoters of a railroad running from Los Angeles to Salt Lake City divided the site into lots and put it up for public sale on that day. It fetched a total of $265,000. Within six years, Las Vegas was made a city by the state legislature. It wasn't until another generation passed, however, that it became a city in fact as well as in law. In the same year as Vegas' founding, the Colorado River went on one of the greatest floods in its history. Much of southeastern California was inundated, hundreds of thousands of acres of farmland lost. The flood provided the political impetus for a compact among the states along the Colorado, providing for construction of dams and allotments of water.

These negotiations were supervised by the then U.S. Secretary of Commerce Herbert Hoover and the actual construction began during his presidency. The largest dam in the project, at Black Canyon, was called Hoover Dam.

Its opening in 1936 redefined the destiny of the Southwest, providing electric power to support the coming tide of population into the area. It also, incidentally, cranked up the juice for downtown Las Vegas, an area that would come to be known as Glitter Gulch. Its bright, animated casino signs illuminated the desert for a 100 miles around. While gambling had been legalized in 1931, the full impact also didn't come to Las Vegas until the big dam came on line.

The town quickly became a weekend getaway for Los Angeles residents, a place for quickie weddings, divorces, crap games or most anything else one had in mind. The action, however, was concentrated downtown. That era ended with the opening of The Strip, south of the city on Las Vegas Boulevard South, in the late 40s. That changed everything. Within a few years, The Strip, greased by Mob money, had become the center of the American entertainment industry. While old time vaudevillians dreamed of "playing the Palace" in New York, the new pinnacle of show business was being a Vegas headliner on The Strip. Underwritten by gambling profits, big name entertainment became the norm, along with a daring innovation imported from Europe, bare-breasted musical revues.

Most luxury hotels were built with a desert theme: Sahara, Dunes, Sands, Desert Inn, Aladdin. They all featured big illuminated signs out front announcing the attractions in their showrooms and prices that were a bargain by any measure. As glitzy as they were, many of these first generation of hotel-casinos are only memories today. They were torn down and replaced by a new round of hotels that drew their inspiration from every geographic area and era of history. Visitors can participate in themed fantasies that take them from ancient Rome to Egypt, from a pirate island to New York City, from Arthurian England to Monte Carlo, from the classic stars of MGM to a pair of magicians with white tigers. Entire amusement parks are housed within these places, as well as dueling ships, circus acts, conventions and bar mitzvahs.

As gambling proliferates around the country, Las Vegas is going through the most profitable economic cycle in its history. It seems that an entirely new market got a small taste of the Vegas experience when gaming came to their own hometowns. That left them hungry to see the real thing and Vegas was eager to oblige. An unprecedented construction spree has transformed the city once again.

LAS VEGAS: ON THE STRIP

In this area, hotels are inseparable from casinos. This is where casino operators first learned that the best way to keep gamblers profitably engaged was to offer so many diversions under one roof that they wouldn't want to leave. That sounds deceptively simple now but it took a while for the concept to catch on. Now the Strip hotels are more like regional shopping malls, offering every conceivable amenity. It once was thought that other attractions would divert attention away from the gaming tables. As it turned out, however, patrons are more likely to put in more time in the casino if they don't have to leave the premises to find other things to do or to chauffeur other members of their family around town. So hotel and casino became one humungous package.

In general, the Strip hotels accept $2 bets at their tables and up to a maximum of $2,000. Baccarat usually involves a $10 minimum. Virtually every leading hotel offers an upscale Italian restaurant, a steak house, a mid-priced Chinese restaurant, a New York-style deli, a Los Angeles-style coffeeshop and a bargain basement buffet. Occasionally, you will also find French or Japanese eating places, too. The Strip begins just south of the city limits, at Sahara Avenue and has gradually pushed further and further south. Hotel-casinos are listed going north to south along its length.

 Sahara, 2535 Las Vegas Boulevard South, (702) 737-2111. At the top of The Strip, the Sahara is one of the first of the mega-sized hotel-casinos. Renovated and enlarged, although no longer up to the quality of some of the newer places. 2,000 rooms, two pools, shops. Showroom and lounge. Thirty-one blackjack tables, 1,000 slots, five craps tables. 200-seat race and sports book with thirty screens.

 Circus Circus, 2880 Las Vegas Boulevard South, (702) 734-0410. This is the one that changed Las Vegas. The first family-oriented hotel-casino on The Strip and the operation that everyone else has tried to emulate. The circus acts are free and run daily, 11 a.m. to midnight. There is also a carnival midway. Rock bottom prices for the 2,793 rooms and various eating places. Eighty-eight blackjack tables, 2,700 slots, six craps tables, 274-seat race and sports book with thirty screens.

 Riviera, 2901 Las Vegas Boulevard South, (702) 734-5110. Another of the old-line Strip holdovers, renovated and enlarged to 2,073 rooms. Lots of luxury touches in rooms and restaurants, but the high-rollers generally stay elsewhere now. Revue-type shows. Ninety blackjack tables, 2,000 slots.

VIOLET MATTSCHECK, WINNER OF $3 MILLION IN SHUFFLE MASTER GAMING'S LET IT RIDE—THE TOURNA-
MENT, WITH A MERMAID AT THE RIVIERA HOTEL & CASINO. (AP WIDE WORLD, SCOTT HARRISON)

 Sheraton Desert Inn, 3145 Las Vegas Boulevard South, (702)
733-4444. Several years of decline followed the death of its odd
former owner, Howard Hughes. But Sheraton spruced up the
Desert Inn and once again, it is a top notch resort. More of an
emphasis on outdoor activities than in nearby Strip properties.
Golf course, health spa, tennis, saunas, jogging track. Assortment of fine restaurants and name entertainment in the showroom. It is also slightly smaller with just 821 rooms. Its casino
has twenty-six blackjack tables, 450 machines, eight craps tables,
forty-seat sports book with twelve screens.

 Treasure Island, 3300 Las Vegas Boulevard South, (702)894-
7111. The main attraction is Buccaneer Bay, where a simulated
battle between the pirate ship *Hispaniola* and the British Navy's

HMS Brittania takes place in front of the casino. With thirty-six stories, Treasure Island features a shopping promenade, a spa and a number of places to dine, including The Black Spot Grille, The Lookout Cafe, Seven Seas Snack Bar and Sweet Revenge Ice Cream Parlor. Nightly entertainment includes the Cirque Du Soleil. The casino offers over 2,100 slots, 570 video poker machines, fifty-two blackjack tables, seven craps tables, eight roulette tables and twelve video blackjack machines. Pai-gow poker, caribbean stud poker and baccarat is also available.

 Mirage, 3400 Las Vegas Boulevard South, (702) 791-7111. The first of the new breed of casinos of the '90s. A tourist attraction in itself with tiger exhibits, dolphin tanks and volcanoes that periodically erupt. The Mirage lobby doubles as a tropical rain forest with a waterfall at its center. Siegfried and Roy, whose magic act is built around the tigers, put on the most popular show in town. There is also a spa, two inter-connected pools,

shopping, and luxury rooms with a South Seas theme. Eight restaurants, serving everything from Left Bank French to left coast pizza. The vast casino features 100 blackjack tables, 2,200 slots, twelve craps tables, and an entirely separate room for baccarat.

Harrah's Las Vegas, 3475 Las Vegas Boulevard South, (702) 369-5008. More modest than most of its big name competitors on The Strip, this is a greatly expanded former Holiday Inn. Showboat theme with a whistle that actually toots loudly every so often. Moderately priced in its rooms, entertainment, restaurants and its betting limit ($1,000 maximum). Fifty-four blackjack tables, 1,800 slots, six craps tables, 155 seats in the sports book with twenty-five screens. Good video bingo operation.

Flamingo Hilton, 3555 Las Vegas Boulevard South, (702) 733-3111. The Strip original and Bugsy Siegel's monument to wretched excess. It's been overhauled quite a bit since its lamentable 1947 opening which led to his untimely demise. Not much of Siegel's hotel remains but Hilton is a far gentler landlord than the Mob. Its big sign is still one of the brightest in the area and at 3,642 rooms it is among the town's biggest. Lots of spa and pool amenities. Thirty-nine blackjack tables, 1,600 slots, eight craps tables, twenty-five seat sports book with two screens.

 Caesar's Palace, 3560 Las Vegas Boulevard South, (702) 731-7110. The paradigm of the Vegas Hotel in the '70s. One of the first with a themed motif throughout, setting the bar for amenities above everything that went before; marbled rooms, gushing fountains, lushly landscaped pools and top of the line prices. Big name entertainment, arena set up for outdoor events, giant movie screen. Some genuinely excellent restaurants, with prices to match. 1,500 rooms. Three separate casinos; the intimate Palace Court is for the patricians, the Roman Forum for the plebeians, and the Olympic Casino for the sports nuts. The latter boasts that it can show any televised sports event from anywhere and its sports book can seat 547 people in front of thirty-eight giant screens. It is the ultimate for this branch of gambling. The Olympic also has thirty blackjack tables, 1,400 slots, three craps tables. The Roman Forum is slightly larger, with thirty-seven blackjack tables and nine craps tables, but has only 600 slots. The Palace Court concentrates on high stakes roulette, baccarat and pai-gow poker.

 Bally's Las Vegas, 3645 Las Vegas Boulevard South, (702) 739-4111. This was the site of the original MGM Grand, built in the mid '70s and taken over by Bally's in the following decade. Its shopping arcade is the largest in town and its outdoor recreation area also is huge, with both men's and women's health clubs. The hotel has 2,813 rooms. Broad range of restaurants, top name entertainment, comedy club. Eight-four blackjack tables, 1,000 slots, eleven craps tables, and a race and sports book.

 Monte Carlo Resort, 3770 Las Vegas Boulevard South, (702) 730-7777. One of the newer, mid-90s resorts, built along a French theme. Five swimming pools. 3,014 rooms. On the site of the defunct Dunes hotel, one of the pioneering legends on The Strip. Also being developed on the same property is the Bellagio, which will resemble an Italian seacoast village. The scheduled opening date for that hotel is 1998.

 MGM Grand, 3799 Las Vegas Boulevard South, (702) 891-1111. The reconstituted MGM, with its movie star theme, is even more spectacular than the original. There are 5,005 rooms and it bills

THE MGM GRAND SHINES AT NIGHT. (COURTESTY OF THE MGM GRAND)

itself as the world's largest hotel. It features a thirty-three-acre theme amusement park (added admission), as well as a youth game center. At 170,000 square feet and 3,500 slots, it's the biggest casino in town.

 Tropicana, 3801 Las Vegas Boulevard South, (702) 739-2222. Another of the old-line Strip operations from the '50s, although when it opened, it represented the far southern end of action. Expanded several times to 1,900 rooms and featuring the usual swimming and health club facilities plus the standard range of restaurants. Forty blackjack tables, 1,100 slots, eight craps tables, sports book with thirty seats and eleven screens.

 Excalibur, 3850 Las Vegas Boulevard South, (702) 597-7700. Opened in 1990, this is built on a Camelot theme, with figures from King Arthur's court wandering about the premises. There are jousting matches, a Renaissance fair, troubadors, a twice-nightly pageant about the Age of Chivalry. Restaurants and the 4,000 rooms also follow the theme. Owned by the Circus Circus operation, this is one of the room and restaurant bargains of Las Vegas. Seventy-eight blackjack tables, 2,600 slots, six craps tables, 250 seats sports book with sixteen screens.

 Luxor, 3900 Las Vegas Boulevard South, (702) 262-4454. Shaped like a gigantic glass pyramid, it is ancient Egypt come to the sands of Nevada. Another of the '90s theme creations, with a replica of King Tut's tomb in the atrium lobby. Its forty-foot high beacon atop the pyramid has become a local landmark. Promoters claim it is the most powerful concentrated beam of light in existence. There are 4,407 rooms, with a good pool and health club area. 2,100 slots, and 109 gaming tables.

THE LUXOR, SHAPED LIKE A GIGANTIC GLASS PYRAMID, IS ANCIENT EGYPT COME TO THE SANDS OF NEVADA. (REUTERS/CORBIS-BETTMANN)

FIREWORKS ERUPT OVER THE NEW YORK, NEW YORK HOTEL & CASINO DURING THE GRAND OPENING.
(ARCHIVE PHOTOS)

 New York, New York, 3790 Las Vegas Boulevard South, (702) 740-6969. A fantasy reproduction of Manhattan and its top tourist attractions. The Empire State Building, the Statue of Liberty, the Brooklyn Bridge. Built to scale, it is an immpressive sight. The Empire State replica, which houses the hotel, is 525-feet tall with forty-eight stories. The Brooklyn Bridge extends 300 feet. The casino itself is done as a vision of Central Park. A Coney Island style roller coaster encircles the grounds, which may be bad news for those sensitive to noise.

LAS VEGAS: ALSO ON THE STRIP

 The Stardust, at 3000 Las Vegas Boulevard South, (702) 732-6111. ˙One of the veterans of The Strip, with an enormous sign that has been since a landmark since the 1950s. 2,341 rooms, most of them at bargain rates. Poker room is highly regarded.

 Imperial Palace, at 3535 Las Vegas Boulevard South, (702) 731-3311. Chinese theme, classic car collection, visitors complain of a confusing layout. 2,700 rooms.

Barbary Coast, at 3595 Las Vegas Boulevard South, (702) 737-7111. A modest operation surrounded by its gigantic mid-Strip competitors. 200 rooms and a turn-of-the-century San Francisco theme. A rather quiet alternative for the area.

Aladdin, at 3667 Las Vegas Boulevard South, (702) 736-0111. Arabian Nights theme. One of the showplaces when it opened in the 1970s, but in spite of several additions and renovations it is no longer one of the top hotel-casinos. 1,100 rooms.

Hacienda, at 3950 Las Vegas Boulevard South, (702) 739-8911. Moderately priced, at the southern end of the strip, friendly towards low-end players. 1,140 rooms.

AN EXTERIOR VIEW OF THE ALADDIN. (AP WIDE WORLD, LENNOX MCLENDON)

LAS VEGAS: OFF-THE-STRIP

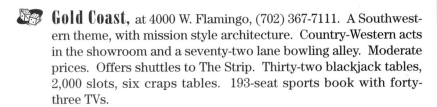

Gold Coast, at 4000 W. Flamingo, (702) 367-7111. A Southwestern theme, with mission style architecture. Country-Western acts in the showroom and a seventy-two lane bowling alley. Moderate prices. Offers shuttles to The Strip. Thirty-two blackjack tables, 2,000 slots, six craps tables. 193-seat sports book with forty-three TVs.

Palace Station, at 2411 W. Sahara, (702) 367-2411. Small, inexpensive, free shuttle service to The Strip. Only 457 rooms, which makes it manageable by Vegas standards. Thirty blackjack tables, 1,700 slots, four craps tables. 200-seat sports book with forty-two TVs. Famous for its bingo room which is well attended by the locals.

Maxim, at 160 E. Flamingo, (702) 731-4300. Good value for those wanting to be close to The Strip. The Maxim is just a block away and is a lot quieter and friendlier than some of the neighboring behemoths. 795 rooms, with most of the amenities of the larger places. Twenty-six blackjack tables, 681 slots, three craps tables. Eleven TVs in the sports book.

197

Las Vegas Hilton, at 3000 Paradise, (702) 732-5111. Still the biggest of the off-Strip hostelries, although no longer the largest in town, a title it held for two decades. There are 3,174 rooms in the thirty-story structure and its showroom books the big-name acts. Luxurious touches in the rooms, spa and restaurants. Thirty-eight blackjack tables, 1,100 slots, seven craps tables. Big sports book with forty-six large screen TVs.

 Rio Suites, east of the Strip, on Flamingo Road at I-15, (702) 252-7777. This Brazilian-themed place is a local favorite. Opened in 1990, it is noted for its large rooms at reasonable prices and its bountiful buffet. Las Vegas residents recommend it for out-of-town visitors. 1,551 rooms.

LAS VEGAS: DOWNTOWN

This area has changed just as profoundly as The Strip in the 90s. The historic core of the city and its casinos, Fremont Street was on a downward slope, with the most prominent signs being ones that read: "Checks cashed." It was perceived as unsafe, seedy and distinctly unfashionable. But the downtown casinos, in an uncharacteristic show of cooperation, decided that they had to act together in order to survive.

So they came up with an unusual strategy, The Frontier Street Experience. This is a wall of moving light that runs the length of the entire district, through five blocks and eight casinos. Hourly shows send the lights off in different patterns and shapes to a musical accompaniment. The total cost was $70 million, shared by the casinos, the city and tourists who paid an additional hotel tax. Although the light display runs against the prevailing casino philosophy, ("Keep 'em inside and playing whatever you do") the casino owners recognized that if downtown were to come back it had to create a safe and attractive outdoors environment. As a result, two of the downtown hotels have recently concluded major expansions and another, Main Street Station, reopened in 1996 after being shut down for four years.

The downtown casinos are noted for being moderately-priced and friendly, aimed at the average traveler rather than the high roller. Lots of slots and dealers who engage you in semi-friendly chit-chat. The entertainment is generally of the Country-Western, lounge act or bare bones revue variety, but that is definitely not the main attraction in this area.

 California, at 12 Ogden Street, just off the casino center, (702) 385-1222. Although it's called the California Hotel, the decor is Hawaiian. Go figure. (This is also not the place the Eagles were

GAMBLERS COLLECT THEIR BETS AT A DOWNTOWN CASINO IN LAS VEGAS. (AP WIDE WORLD, LENNOX McCLENDON)

singing about it in their song hit—the Hotel California, where you could check out anytime you liked but you could never leave.) 650 rooms and twenty-three stories. Twenty-four blackjack tables, 1,000 slots, six craps tables. Small sports book, separate lounge for Keno.

Fitzgerald's, at 301 E. Fremont, (702) 388-2400. Finishing up a 600-room expansion which doubled its size to more than 1,200. Before the new generation of Strip mega-hotels were built in the mid '90s, it was the tallest building in Nevada. Irish theme, much like the one in Reno. Big attraction is the slot machines which promise a 101-percent payback and are advertised as "the loosest in Vegas."

Four Queens, at 202 E. Fremont, (702) 385-4011. It has the local branch of the Ripley Believe-It-or-Not Museum and a nice

little showroom which features jazz performances. A New Orleans theme. 709 rooms, exercise room. Twenty-seven blackjack tables, 955 slots, six craps tables.

Fremont, at 200 E. Fremont, (702) 385-3232. Budget operation in the center of the casino district. Twenty-six blackjack tables, 1,000 slots, four craps tables. Good sports book with 140 seats and twenty TVs.

Golden Nugget, at 129 E. Fremont, (702) 385-7111. Exceptional hotel for the downtown area, with many of the touches associated with the pricier Strip operations. A good value for bargain hunters. Spa and pool, large, bright rooms. 1,907 rooms. Forty-six blackjack tables, 1,100 slots, six craps tables. Sixty seat sports book with twenty-seven screens. Baccarat room.

Binion's Horseshoe, at 128 E. Fremont, (702) 382-1600. A small place celebrated for big money legends in its past. Tales abound of no-limit bettors who breezed in and won a quarter million on one roll of the dice. 339 rooms, with an older section and a high rise addition with a rooftop pool. Big, crowded, noisy casino with fifty-three blackjack tables, 865 slots, fourteen craps tables. The World Series of poker is held here and the tables in that room are legendary. Sports book with 162 seats and twenty-one screens.

 Lady Luck, at 206 N. Third, just off the casino district, (702) 477-3000. A bit more secluded, but just as lively as its competitors downtown. 791 rooms in two towers, many poolside rooms, some with indoor Jacuzzis. The casino is one block long and features the largest dance floor in town, at 1,000 square feet. Noted for its bargain promotions and also for a casino school for beginners. Twenty-four blackjack tables, 1,000 slots, four craps tables.

 Las Vegas Club, at 18 E. Fremont, (702) 385-1664. Built by a diehard Brooklyn Dodgers fan, the hotel boasts the most extensive collection of baseball memorabilia outside of Cooperstown. The lineup of autographed World Series bats is the largest in private hands anywhere. Sports theme is followed in other aspects of the hotel, which recently added a twenty-story tower. The casino promotes the most liberal blackjack rules anywhere, permitting players to double down on any two cards or throw in their hand after two cards for only half the original bet. Fourteen tables, 650 slots, thirty-seat sports book with six large screens.

 Plaza, at 1 Main Street, (702) 386-2110. One of the newer hotels downtown, with 1,000 rooms, good sports facilities, including heated pool, jogging track and (rare for this location) tennis courts. Situated inside the Amtrak terminal. Shopping arcade, showroom. Twenty-six blackjack tables, 1,500 slots, five craps tables. 170 seats in the sports book with thirty-four TVs.

LAUGHLIN

The town is situated at the southern tip of the state, wedged into the angle between California and Arizona. It is ninety-five miles south of Las Vegas, by way of U.S. 95 and Nevada 163. Also accessible from I-40, at Needles, California; forty miles by way of northbound U.S. 95 and Nevada 163.

When the Davis Dam was being built on the Colorado River in 1966, a Nevadan named Don Laughlin decided to open a bar and casino across from construction headquarters, in Bullhead City, Arizona. He wanted to call it Riverside. But postal authorities rejected that name

Small-scale Casinos for the Casual Traveler

The following casinos are located along I-80.

- Wendover, just across the Utah line on the main road from Reno to Salt Lake City. The town is actually cut in half by the border and was once a supply base for cars racing at the nearby Bonneville Salt Flats.

  Peppermill Inn and Casino, (702) 664-2255.

  Silver Smith Casino and Resort, (702) 664-2231.

- Wells, fifty-nine miles west of Wendover at U.S. 93. Named for its wells that replenished pioneers on the Humboldt Trail.

  Four-Way Cafe and Casino, (702) 752-334.

  Nevada Travel Center and Casino, (702) 752-3384.

- Elko, thirty miles west of Wells, famed for its Basque Festival in July and its Cowboy Poetry Gathering in January. At the center of the state's leading ranching area.

  Red Lion Motor Inn and Casino, at 2065 Idaho Street, (702) 738-2111.

- Battle Mountain, seventy-two miles west of Elko, named for a skirmish between settlers and Native Americans in the 1860s. It is still the supply point for a vast mining area that stretches to the south.

  Jackpot Owl Club, at 72 E. Front Street, (702) 635-5155.

- Winnemucca, fifty-one miles west of Battle Mountain, a key railroad stop for the mines. Named for a Paiute chief. This is also a Basque community and is surrounded by sheep-raising country.

  Red Lion Inn and Casino, at 741 W. Winnemucca Boulevard, (702) 623-2565.

- Verdi, eight miles west of Reno, is an old lumber camp in the Sierra, right at the California border.

  The Boomtown Hotel and Casino, which started off as a truck stop, now has a good-sized casino, with thirty-six blackjack tables and 1,000 slots.

because of confusion with all the other Riversides in the country. Laughlin then offered Casino as his choice, but that too was turned down. Finally, the post office sensibly decided to call it Laughlin.

For a time, it seemed that the founder would have his new town pretty much to himself. There were no Interstates in the vicinity, no jet airports. But Laughlin had discovered something. The big Las Vegas hotels and casinos had become fat and happy in the 1970s, and were slowly pricing themselves out of the range of blue collar workers. Laughlin decided to target that market. He deliberately built his parking lots to accomodate trailers and RVs, set his rates at rock bottom, and made sure that his dealers were always friendly towards beginners.

As the impounded lakes along the Colorado River took off as a boating area, Laughlin began to boom. It also boasted that its winter climate was an average of ten degrees warmer than Las Vegas. Its fulltime population is still negligible, but hotel occupancy runs in the thousands each weekend. Several big Vegas hotels have established branches here, but the tradition of low prices and down home ambience still holds. There are also free boat rides across the river to Arizona, tours of the Davis Dam and boating on Lake Mohave, which the dam created.

With the exception of the Avi Hotel Casino, owned by the Mojave indians, the casinos in Laughlin are clustered along Casino Drive, which parallels the Colorado River. All are open daily, twenty-four hours.

The Mohave have made their home along the Colorado River for about 300 years. They encountered early Spanish explorers, but their lands were so remote that their lives were only lightly touched. The agricultural people were centered around the Black Canyon of the Colorado (the site of Hoover Dam) and the rock formation that gives the town of Needles, California, its name. Reservations were established for them in 1864, and while the Fort Mojave lands are primarily in Arizona, the tribe runs the Avi Hotel-Casino in the Nevada resort across the river.

 Avi Hotel Casino, *(Fort Mojave Tribal Council).* 10000 Parkway, ninety-five miles south of Las Vegas, by way of U.S. 95 and Nevada 163. (702) 535-5555.

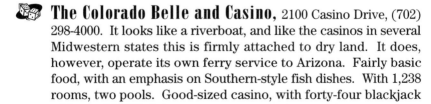 **The Colorado Belle and Casino,** 2100 Casino Drive, (702) 298-4000. It looks like a riverboat, and like the casinos in several Midwestern states this is firmly attached to dry land. It does, however, operate its own ferry service to Arizona. Fairly basic food, with an emphasis on Southern-style fish dishes. With 1,238 rooms, two pools. Good-sized casino, with forty-four blackjack tables and 1,200 slots.

Edgewater Hotel and Casino, at 2020 S. Casino Drive, (702) 298-2453. There are 1,492 rooms and thirty-two lanes in its bowling alley, which also features a restaurant and pro shop. Medical facilities on site. There are thirty-two blackjack tables, 1,200 machines, sports book with twenty TVs.

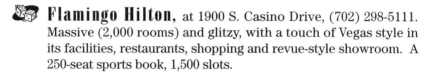

Flamingo Hilton, at 1900 S. Casino Drive, (702) 298-5111. Massive (2,000 rooms) and glitzy, with a touch of Vegas style in its facilities, restaurants, shopping and revue-style showroom. A 250-seat sports book, 1,500 slots.

Golden Nugget Casino, at 2300 Casino Drive, (702) 298-7111. Tropical flora and fauna throughout the place with a rain forest theme in the atrium lobby. One of the smaller hotels with 300 rooms and the casino built along the same lines: thirteen blackjack tables, 860 slots.

Harrah's Laughlin, at 2900 Casino Drive, (702) 298-4600. The only Laughlin casino right on the river, featuring a private beach and the theme of a Mexican-style resort in its rooms and restaurants. Water sports facilities, including jet skis and boat rentals. Cabaret shows, as well as an RV service center. 1,000 slots, which are the main attraction in its 40,000-square foot casino.

Ramada Express, at 2121 Casino Drive, (702) 298-4200. Built on a railroad theme, with rides from the parking lot to the station-style hotel on a miniature train. Even the pool is shaped like a locomotive and the gift shops sell railroad memorabilia. Twenty-six blackjack tables, 1,000 slots, only racing in the sports book.

The Riverside Casino and Resort, 1650 Casino Drive, (702) 298-2535. The Laughlin original, expanded to 660 rooms. Two outdoor pools, massive RV lot, shopping arcade, name entertainment. The place boasts that beef for its restaurants is raised on a nearby casino-owned ranch. The casino is medium-sized with twenty-eight blackjack tables, 1,300 slots, a bingo room, a glass-enclosed poker room and a sports book.

MESQUITE

A former Mormon farming colony along the Virgin River, this is now a gambling stopover for drivers coming from southern Utah on I-15.

Players Island Resort Spa, (702) 346-7529. Opened in 1995, this is a 486-room hotel in a nine-story tower. The hotel also has a pool, small spa, tennis courts, a golf course and two restaurants.

An Added Attraction

Minden is a beautiful village, fourteen miles south of Carson City at the base of the Sierra. The Carson Valley Inn is a surprisingly scenic getaway, with a 160-room hotel, and a small casino, with nine blackjack tables and 370 machines. This is a place where Nevadans get away when they feel like ducking the crowds. (702) 782-9711.

 Virgin River Hotel and Casino, (702) 346-7777. A sprawling 723-room complex over two floors, with two pools, two movie theaters, video arcade, one restaurant and a buffet.

RENO

Before there ever was a Reno, people liked to linger on the site. It was then known as Truckee Meadows and travelers heading west could stop along the river, feed their stock, regard the bulk of the Sierras straight ahead and gather strength for the final rush to California. The Donner Party lingered here a few days too long in 1846 and was trapped in the snow at the pass that bears its name, now the main Interstate route from Reno to San Francisco.

Reno itself didn't come into existence until twenty-one years later. It was a railroad center, created out of open fields which were divided into lots and sold at auction. The vacant land fetched a high price because arrival of the railroad made it the main shipping and supply point for the Comstock Lode. Later, Reno served the same function for the major strikes at Tonopah and Goldfield. By the first part of the twentieth century, it was a fairly prosperous financial and transportation center and the seat of the state university. Then in 1931 came the twin upheavals of liberalized divorce and gambling.

Almost overnight Reno became a national symbol of wickedness. Eastern newspapers editorialized sternly about the moral decay betokened by the two new laws. Reno, as the biggest city in the state, was the focus of their indignation. Travelers to the West wondered earnestly whether it was safe to leave the train here. But Reno's casino area was always fairly much limited to a strip of a few downtown blocks along Virginia Street while its marriage chapels were always far busier than its divorce courts.

In recent years, it has added new casinos. As far as gaming is concerned, however, it has been eclipsed by Las Vegas, which is now also the state's largest city. Reno always believed in diversifying its economy and it has become known as a winter sports center as well as a solid business town. Moreover, its National Bowling Stadium, opened in 1995, with eighty lanes, a $4 million video scoring system and IMAX theater, has turned Reno into a tournament center for the sport.

Sparks, which adjoins Reno on the east, grew up around the Southern Pacific rail yards, which were moved there in 1904. In earlier days, all transcontinental trains stopped in Sparks. Enthusiastic gamblers could jump on the local, go into Reno for twenty minutes and then run to board the main line again. That service is no longer offered. Now the fourth largest city in the state, Sparks is politically distinct from its larger neighbor. It has developed its own casino district, too, along Victorian Avenue.

The Reno casinos offer the entire spectrum of gaming—slots, tables, poker rooms, bingo and sports books. Even the largest casinos have tables that accept $2 bets, with $1,000 the usual maximum.

RENO: THE TOP OF THE LINE

 Bally's, at 2500 E. Second Street, (702) 789-2000. Resort hotel with 2,000 rooms. Fifty-lane bowling alley, tennis courts, large swimming pool, shopping arcade. Six restaurants, lounge, comedy club. Seventy-five blackjack tables, 800 slots, six craps tables, sports book with six screens.

 Circus Circus, at 500 N. Virginia, (702) 329-0711. An enormous branch of the Las Vegas family-oriented resort, with more than 1,600 rooms, some priced as low as $29 a night. Circus acts performing constantly. Moderately priced restaurants. Sixty blackjack tables, 2,500 slots, four craps tables, sports book with six screens in the lounge.

 El Dorado Hotel and Casino, at 345 N. Virginia, (702) 786-5700. Resort hotel with 834 rooms, many in a recently built twenty-five story tower are more luxurious. Imaginative assortment of restaurants, top buffet, popular cabaret club. Sixty-five blackjack tables, 1,500 slots, four craps tables, twenty-six seat sports book.

 Flamingo Hilton, at 255 N. Sierra, (702) 785-7000. Big and flashy branch of the pioneer casino on the Vegas Strip. 604 rooms makes it a little smaller than others in this group. Rooftop

Harrah's

This is the name that is synonymous with Reno, the base of a gaming-resort empire that is now nationwide. William Harrah came to Reno in 1937 and opened a bingo parlor with a borrowed $500. Trained as a mechanical engineer, the Depression made it necessary to follow other pursuits. Always fascinated by historic cars, Harrah began investing in them with his casino profits and used them as promotional tools. After several years, though, the cars were taking up more space than the casino. Harrah's National Automobile Museum has become a free-standing facility, at 10 S. Lake Street. It is one of Reno's top attractions, in additon to being one of the best of its kind in the world. The hotel, which was recently renovated, has 500 rooms, a health club, large pool and an attached convention center. Harrah's also features an outstanding buffet, a wide range of restaurants and name entertainment.

restaurants offers exceptional views of the Sierra. Comedy club. Thirty-six blackjack tables, 900 slots, three craps tables, fifty-four seat sports book with twenty-six televisions.

 Harrah's, at 219 N. Center Street, (702) 786-3232. Seventy blackjack tables, 2,000 slots, eight craps tables, 120 seats sports book and sixty-seat racing book, poker room.

RENO: THE MID-SIZED CASINOS

 Atlantis Casino Resort, at 3800 S. Virginia Street, (702) 825-4700. Formerly the Clarion Hotel, the resort has been renovated and expanded with tropical theme and 600 rooms. Several rooms include Jacuzzis. Health club, large pool. 1,000 slots.

 Club Cal-Neva, at 38 E. Second, (702) 323-1046. A branch of the Lake Tahoe operation, aimed at beginners and moderate players. Thirty blackjack tables, 1,200 slots, four craps tables, 250-seat race and sports book.

 Fitzgerald's Hotel Casino, at 255 N. Virginia Street. Large scale renovation of the 350-room hotel concluded in 1996. Irish theme, located right at the famous "Biggest Little City" arch. Moderate priced restaurants. Ten blackjack tables, 2,500 slots, two craps tables.

DEALER OKOHA MEYERS DEALS A TABLE GAME CALLED "BEAT THE DEALER," A VARIATION OF BLACKJACK, AT ATLANTIS CASINO RESORT IN RENO, NEVADA. (AP WIDE WORLD, TIM DNN)

Peppermill Hotel Casino, at 2707 S. Virginia, (702) 826-2121. In an outlying area, close to mall shopping. Large pool, free shuttle to downtown, fitness center. Twenty-nine blackjack tables, 550 slots, three craps tables.

Riverboat Hotel and Casino, at 34 W. Second, (702) 323-8877. Mississippi riverboat and Southern theme followed through in room decor and restaurants. Moderate prices. Thirteen blackjack tables, 380 slots, one craps table.

The Virginian, at 140 N. Virginia, (702) 329-4664. Typical of the newer Reno casinos, right in the heart of the traditional downtown district. Moderate prices, especially at breakfast. Eighteen blackjack tables, 460 slots, one craps table.

RENO: IN SPARKS

John Ascuaga's Nugget, at 1125 B Street, (702) 356-3300. A Sparks landmark, with 1,400 rooms in sixteen stories, rooftop swimming pool, celebrity showroom, local ownership. Large assortment of restaurants, most of them moderately priced. One of the largest casinos in the area. Forty blackjack tables, 1,400 slots, eight craps tables, seventy-five seat sports book.

 Silver Club, at 1040 B Street, (702) 358-4771. Themed to fit in with the Victorian surroundings of the area. 200-room motor inn attached to the casino. Oversized spaces to accommodate RVs. Good buffets. Thirteen blackjack tables, 630 slots, one craps table, 150 seats in sports book.

New Mexico

Casino operations are run by Native American tribes. Thorough-bred racing is also available. For state lottery information, contact the New Mexico State Lottery.

 New Mexico State Lottery, 4511 Osuna Road SE, Albuquerque 87109, (505)342-7600. Sales: $67 million. Proceeds: $13 million. 100% education.

ACOMITA

Operated by the fabled mesa-top Acoma pueblo, one of the oldest continuously inhabited places in the United States. Established around 1200, Acoma has a rich heritage, with a well-developed tourist industry as well as interests in grazing, mining and crafts. It is regarded as one of the more culturally conservative pueblos.

 Sky City Casino, *(Pueblo of Acoma).* Seventy miles west of Albuquerque on I-40. (505)552-6604.

ALBUQUERQUE

 Downs at Albuquerque, thoroughbred track. At the State Fairgrounds, east from downtown on Central Avenue. January–April. (505)266-5555.

 Isleta Gaming Palace, *(Pueblo of Isleta).* 11000 Broadway SE, in the southern suburbs. (505)869-2514.

Isleta Pueblo is situated just south of the Albuquerque metro-politan area. It was on the same site when Coronado visited in 1540. The name means "little island" and is derived from its position along the Rio Grande. During the revolt against Spain in 1681, it was burned and its inhabitants fled to live with the Hopi. In 1718 they returned and built the pueblo that stands now.

 Sandia Casino, *(Pueblo of Sandia).* Just north of the city, along I-25. (505)897-2173.

Sandia was one of eight Tiwa communities that occupied this portion of the Rio Grande at the time of the first European exploration in 1540. Most of them were burned in the uprising against Spain and their occupants fled to safety with neighboring tribes. Sandia's residents didn't return until 1792 and then, 111 years after its destruction, the pueblo was rebuilt.

BERNALILLO

Santa Ana was one of the Keresan pueblos, built in the mesa land west of the Rio Grande. In the eighteenth century, the residents began moving to the river to raise their crops. Eventually, a new community was built there and the old Santa Ana was abandoned. It is now used for ceremonial occasions.

 Santa Ana Star Casino, *(Pueblo of Santa Ana).* 54 Jemez Dam Canyon Road, thirty miles north of Albuquerque by way of I-25 and New Mexico 44. (505)867-3489.

DULCE

This northernmost Apache community is occupied by the Jicarilla branch. The name means "little basket." The skillful craftwork indicates strong influences from the neighboring Pueblo communities, with whom they were on peaceful terms. Raids on wagon trains along the Santa Fe trail led to reprisals by the U.S. government, however, and the Jicarilla were pushed south and west, out of Colorado. After thirty years of dislocation, they were placed on this reservation in 1887. They have a well-developed tourism industry and their crafts remain a major attraction.

 Apache Nugget Casino, *(Jicarilla Apache Tribe).* Eighty-five miles east of Farmington, on U.S. 64. (505)759-3777.

RUIDOSO

 Ruidoso Downs, thoroughbred track. On U.S. 70, east of the town of Ruidoso, seventy miles west of Roswell. The meet runs from Memorial Day through October. (505)378-4431.

Ruidoso Downs

One of the state's most popular resorts grew up around this track and the summer meets draw spectators from across the Southwest. With the Sacramento Mountains as a backdrop and an art colony in the nearby town this is one of the most picturesque racing venues in the country. Ruidoso Downs originated as a track for quarter horse races from neighboring ranches. Thoroughbreds also race there now, but the track is most famous for hosting all three legs of the triple crown for quarter horses. It culminates in the All American Futurity, held on Labor Day, with a purse of $2 million. The Museum of the Horse, with paintings, sculpture and racing equipment, adjoins the track. It is open daily, 9-5:30, Memorial Day through October; closed Mondays the rest of the year.

SAN JUAN

The first capital of New Mexico was built here by Spanish authorities in 1598. Relations deteriorated as the Europeans sought to end Native American religious practices. A revolt, led by a San Juan religious leader, Pope, drove the Spanish out of New Mexico in 1680 but they returned with a vengeance, burning the pueblos that participated in the rebellion. San Juan then settled into a warm relationship with Spain and was known for its high degree of intermarriage.

 OHKAY Casino, *(Pueblo of San Juan).* Thirty miles north of Santa Fe, by way of U.S. 285 and New Mexico 68. (505)747-1668.

SANTA FE

 Camel Rock Casino, *(Pueblo of Tesuque).* On the northern outskirts of the city. (505)984-8414. A tiny pueblo occupied by a Tiwa people.

One of the smallest of the Tiwa pueblos, numbering only about 100 residents at its peak. The present pueblo dates from 1706.

 Cities of Gold Casino, *(Pueblo of Pojoaque).* Route 11, sixteen miles north of Santa Fe. (505)455-3313.

 The Downs at Santa Fe, thoroughbred track. South on I025, then follow signs. Daily, June to Labor Day. (505)471-3311.

SUNLAND PARK

 Sunland Park, thoroughbred track. On New Mexico 273, northwest of downtown El Paso, Texas by way of I-10, across the Rio Grande bridge. Water skiing shows in the infield lake. January–May. (505)589-1131.

TAOS

The most famous of the New Mexico pueblos, Taos is celebrated as an inspiration for artists and for the purity of its culture. The site, with a creek winding through the center of the community and Mt. Taos as a backdrop, has been a tourist attraction for a century. Before that Taos was a major trade center between the pueblo and Plains tribes and an important station on the Santa Fe Trail.

 Taos Slot Room, *(Pueblo of Taos)*. Seventy-five miles north of Santa Fe, by way of U.S. 285 and New Mexico 68. (505)758-9593.

Oregon

There are six Native American casinos in Oregon for gaming. Oregon voters passed an amendment to their state constitution in 1984 specifically outlining the types of gaming that would be permitted. Video lottery terminals with a maximum of five terminals per merchant are allowed by law. The player has a choice of video keno, video poker or wagering on sporting events. There are over 1,500 locations offering video lottery terminals. For state lottery information, contact the Oregon State Lottery.

 Oregon State Lottery, 500 Airport Road SE, Salem 97301, (503)540-1000. Sales: $345 million. Proceeds: $81 million. 100% Economic Development Fund.

CANYONVILLE

The Umpqua was the name given to a group of small tribes who lived along the Oregon coast and based their livelihood on fishing. But disease so ravaged the tribe that less than 100 survived into the twentieth century. After being placed on the Grande Ronde Reservation in 1856, most became absorbed in the general population.

 Seven Feathers Gaming Resort, *(Cow Creek Band of Umpqua Indians).* 146 Chief Miwaleta Lane, ninety-five miles south of Eugene, on I-5. (503)839-1111.

GRAND RONDE

The Grande Ronde reserve was set up in the 1850s as a home for several small tribes who lived in coastal Oregon. The Chinook, Shasta, Umpqua and Kalapuya all made their homes there and, in the main, struggled to maintain their identities in the face of dwindling numbers.

MARY WIRTA DEALS A WINNING BLACKJACK HAND AT THE SPIRIT MOUNTAIN CASINO IN GRAND RONDE, OREGON. (AP WIDE WORLD, DOUG BEGHTEL)

 Spirit Mountain Gaming, *(Confederated Tribes of the Grande Ronde Indian Community).* Salmon River Highway, thirty-five miles west of Salem by way of Oregon 22 and 16. (503)879-2350.

LINCOLN CITY

Siletz was another of the communities established for coastal tribes, primarily the Chinook. This people, whose identity is preserved in the name of a warm winter wind and a kind of gamefish, lived near the mouth of the Columbia River, in Oregon and Washington. But they couldn't survive the contact with white disease and were scattered among several neighboring tribes by the 1850s.

 Chinook Winds, *(Confederated Tribes of the Siletz Indians of Oregon).* 1777 NW 44th Street, off U.S. 101, twenty-five miles north of Newport. (541)996-5825.

215

THE CONFEDERATED TRIBES OF THE SILETZ INDIANS OWN THE CHINOOK WINDS CASINO IN LINCOLN CITY, OREGON. (AP WIDE WORLD, JACK SMITH)

NORTH BEND

The Coquille community is composed of descendants of several small tribes who once lived in the Coos Bay area, most notably the Coos and the Alsea. Most members are assimilated in the general population. The area is one of the most scenic along the Oregon coast and a highly popular resort area.

 The Mill Casino, *(Coquille Indian Tribe).* 3201 N. Tremont, just north of Coos Bay on U.S. 101. (541)756-8800.

PENDLETON

Besides the Umatilla, the Wallawalla and Cayuse tribes live on this reservation. They have developed successful stock-raising and tourist industries and participate annually in the famed Pendleton Roundup, one of the great Western shows in the country.

 Wildhorse Gaming Resort, *(Confederated Tribes of the Umatilla Indian reservation).* 72777 Highway 331, east of town, off I-84. (541)278-2274.

PORTLAND

 Portland Meadows, thoroughbred track. At 1001 N. Schmeer Road, off Oregon 99E, north of downtown. Daily, October–April. (503)285-9144.

The Pendleton Roundup

The cattle drives from Texas north to the railheads on the Great Plains were long hard pulls for cowboys and livestock alike. While the Pendleton cattle drives didn't cover quite as great a distance, they may have been even more difficult, because a good part of their course was uphill, across the passes of the Rockies.

Pendleton was the center of a vast cattle empire in eastern Oregon throughout the 1880s. The herds were driven to railroad towns in Montana and Wyoming for shipment east. It was a hazardous trip, and a certain camaraderie developed among the cowboys who made it. The drives ended in 1889 when the railroad finally reached Pendleton, and shortly afterwards the country began changing to an agricultural base. But the legacy of the old drives lived on among the old-timers, and in 1910 the town held its first roundup.

It was meant to be part community rodeo and part celebration of the past. It was so well received, however, that in 1912 it became an annual event, held the second full week in September. Native Americans from the adjacent Umadilla Reservation joined in enthusiastically from the start, and Jackson Sundown, a member of that tribe, was one of the winners of the all-around cowboy award. The Roundup has become one of the best-attended events in the West and even runs its own hall of fame. The Roundup events include: rodeo, covered wagon parades, Indian encampment and traditional dances, Old West entertainment and costumed reenactments. For information contact: Pendleton Roundup Offices, P.O. Box 609, Pendleton, Oregon 97801, (800)524-2984. (from *Historic Festivals: A Traveler's Guide,* by George Cantor, Visible Ink Press, 1996)

WARM SPRINGS

The Paiute occupied the eastern slope of the Cascades and Sierra from Oregon all the way to the Mojave Desert of California. Because of the climatic differences that lay across their range, they are generally divided into northern and southern branches. The northern Paiute were a fishing and hunting people and battled with the Wishram for control of northern Oregon for generations. Eventually, both Paiute and Wishram were relocated on the Warm Springs reservation in the scenic country on the slopes of Mount Hood and have built a successful spa resort.

 Indian Head Gaming Center, *(Confederated Tribes of the Warm Springs Reservation).* Forty-five miles southeast of the Mount Hood turnoff from U.S. 26. (541)553-6122

Washington

There are a number of Native American casinos operating in Washington. For state lottery information, contact the Washington State Lottery.

 Washington State Lottery, 814 Fourth Avenue, Olympia 98504, (360)753-1412. Sales: $390 million. Proceeds: $106 million. 100% General fund.

ANACORTES

The Swinomish and Skagit people live on this reservation, which is close to their ancestral homeland along the northern Washington coast. Salmon was their staple food and life was organized around their migration pattern. The reservation was set aside for them in 1855.

 Swinomish Casino, *(Swinomish Indian Tribal Community).* 837 Swinomish Casino Drive, thirty-five miles south of Bellingham, by way of I-5 and Washington 20. (360)293-2691.

AUBURN

 Emerald Downs, thoroughbred track. East of Washington 167, at 15th Street NW; twenty-eight miles south of downtown Seattle. Daily, April–September. (206)931-8400.

The small Muckleshoot reservation, at the edge of suburban sprawl, is laid out in four interlocking squares on the south bank of the Green River. Inhabitants are related to the neighboring Puyallup community.

The Annual Stommish Festival

With its war canoe races and traditional music, games, and dances, the Stommish Festival in Bellingham is one of the most unusual and colorful in the country. It is based on the traditional potlatches of the Northwest, gatherings at which tribes met for a communal feast and exchange of gifts. The festival is usually held the third week of June, but schedule shifts are possible and it is best to call in advance. The Lummi operate a charter boat, manned by tribal members, for cruises through the local waters. A gift shop next to the restaurant carries wool sweaters, baskets, and carvings, characteristic Lummi crafts. For more information call (360)384-1489. (from *North American Indian Landmarks: A Traveler's Guide,* by George Cantor, Visible Ink Press, 1993)

 Muckleshoot Indian Casino, *(Muckleshoot Tribe).* 2602 Auburn Way South, in the eastern suburbs of Tacoma, by way of I-5 and Washington 18. (360)735-2404.

BELLINGHAM

The Lummi occupy what may be the most scenic reservation in the Northwest. It juts into the Strait of Georgia, with views of the Cascades, the port of Bellingham and Olympic Peninsula. The Lummi operate a profitable fishing fleet as well as taking advantage of the tourism possibilities presented by the setting. Their annual Stommish Festival, which celebrates the culture of the Northwest tribes, is a major event.

 Lummi Casino, *(Lummi Nation).* 2559 Lummi View Drive, on the peninsula opposite Bellingham, by way of county roads from the Marietta exit of I-5. (360)758-7559. Offers 300 bingo seats, twenty-three blackjack tables, craps, roulette, seven poker tables, big six tables and red dog tables.

BOW

The Upper Skagit separated from the coastal branch of the tribe and made a living by logging their ancestral lands in the Cascade foothills. Those rights were taken away from them when Washington National Forest was created in 1897 and reservation lands set up, in a more remote area. Many tribal members still work for private logging companies in the area and as agricultural workers. The casino is not on reservation land.

 Harrah's Skagit Valley Casino, *(Upper Skagit Indian Tribe).* 590 Dark Lane, twenty miles south of Bellingham, off I-5. (360)724-7777.

DAVENPORT

The Spokane were a Salishan people who migrated into eastern Washington from British Columbia in the eighteenth century. They were already dwindling in number by the time Lewis and Clark encountered them in 1804 and wars with the U.S. Army in the 1850s further depleted them. The reservation was established in 1881, but construction of Grand Coulee Dam made it impossible for salmon, a staple food, to migrate this far inland. The tribe is highly assimilated.

 Two Rivers Casino, *(Spokane Indian Community).* 6828 B Highway 25 South, thirty-six miles west of Spokane on U.S. 2. (509)722-4009.

DEMING

This tiny community is situated amid the mountain grandeur of the northern Cascades, surrounded by forest.

 Nooksack River Casino, *(Nooksack Indian Tribe).* 5048 Mount Baker Highway, fifteen miles east of Bellingham, on Washington 542. (360)592-5472.

MANSON

Ten tribes who once lived in eastern Washington and Oregon now reside on the one-million acre Colville Reservation, the largest in the state. The Colville, a Salishan-speaking people, constitute the majority but there are also large numbers of Yakima and Nez Perce, including descendants of Chief Joseph's band. The casino is on a scenic portion of Lake Chelan, a recreational area off the reservation.

 Mill Bay Casino, *(Confederated Tribes of the Colville reservation).* 455 E. Wapato Lake Road, fifty miles north of Wenatchee, by way of U.S. 97 and Washington 150. (509)687-2102.

MARYSVILLE

The Tulalip Reserve is situated on a point opposite the port of Everett and is the home of several small Puget Sound tribes who had lost their fishing rights elsewhere. Set up in 1900, the reserve contains several fine nineteenth century mission buildings, as well as beautiful vistas.

 Tulalip Bingo, *(Tulalip Tribes of Washington).* 6330 33rd Avenue NE, just north of Everett on I-5. (360)651-3232.

NEAH BAY

Located at the extreme northwestern corner of the Olympic Peninsula, in one of the most majestic and remote sites in the continental United States. Neah Bay occupies a dramatic site, where the Strait of Juan de Fuca widens to meet the Pacific. The Makah are more closely related to Alaskan tribes than others in Washington, and were adept whalers and seal-hunters. There is a museum of their culture here.

 Makah Bingo, *(Makah Indian Tribe).* Eighty miles west of Port Angeles, on Washington 112. (360)645-2201.

OKANOGAN

On the western edge of the Colville Reservation, in the scenic Okanogan River Valley, at the eastern edge of the Cascades.

 Okanogan Bingo Casino, *(Confederated Tribes of the Colville Reservation).* 41 Appleway Road, ninety-five miles north of Wenatchee, on U.S. 97. (509)687-2102.

ROCHESTER

The Chehalis were a small group living around the Grays Harbor area, to the west of the reservation. They are closely affiliated with the Chinook.

 Chehalis Tribal Lucky Eagle Casino. 12888 188th Street SW, twenty-five miles south of Olympia, on I-5 and U.S. 12. (360)273-2000.

SEQUIM

The Klallam lived along the southern side of the Strait of Juan de Fuca and on Vancouver Island, British Columbia. Removed to reservations elsewhere on the coast, they returned to this area, instead, which is in a rain shadow and differs greatly in climate from the surrounding region. Some small reserves were set aside for them in 1968.

 Seven Cedars Casino, *(Jamestown S'Klallam Tribe).* 270756 Highway 101, seventeen miles east of Port Angeles. (360)681-6717.

SHELTON

Several small coastal tribes live on Squaxin Island, across the water from the state capital of Olympia.

 Little Creek Casino, *(Squaxin Island Tribe).* 91 W. Highway 108, twenty miles north of Olympia, by way of U.S. 101. (360)427-7711.

SPOKANE

 Playfair Racecourse. At N. Altamont and E. Main, east of downtown. July–November. (509)534-0505.

SUQUAMISH

The Suquamish was the name given to a confederacy of tribes in the Puget Sound area. When European settlers arrived, Seattle was the leader of the tribes. Understanding that the numbers opposing him were overwhelming, Seattle saw the best way to secure the interests of his people was to sign a treaty that would give them a semblance of firm borders on an island near their traditional home. Unlike many such treaties, this one was decently respected and the city built by the new-comers was named for the Suquamish chief. The site of his birthplace, Old-Man House, is still preserved here and his grave is located on a hill-side above the Sound.

 Suquamish Bingo. 15347 Suquamish Way, across Puget Sound from Seattle with frequent ferryboat connections. (360)598-1835.

TACOMA

An urban facility run by the Puyallup, whose reservation adjoins Tacoma's eastern border. It contains only thirty-three acres, the rest having been sold off in the previous decades to accommodate urban expansion.

 Puyallup Tribes Bingo Palace, 2002 E. 28th Street. (206)383-1572.

WELLPINIT

 Spokane Indian Casino. Forty-five miles northwest of Spokane, by way of U.S. 2 and Washington 231. (509)258-4581. Located in the middle of the Spokane Reservation.

YAKIMA

 Yakima Meadows, at the Fairgrounds, thoroughbred track. All year. (509)248-3920.

Wyoming

The 1.9 million acre Wind River Reservation in the center of the state is occupied jointly by the Shoshone and Northern Arapaho, who were once bitter enemies. Washakie was the name of a Shoshone chief and it was he who cut the deal with the federal government to secure this tract in the rich Popo Agie Valley in 1872. They were joined there a decade later by the Arapaho who could not adjust to conditions on their alloted reservation in Oklahoma. The tribes operate a profitable stock-raising business. Fort Washakie is also the traditional burial place of Sacajawea, who helped guide the Lewis and Clark expedition through the west. She was born a Shoshone in the Wind River country, was carried off by Sioux raiders, then returned here after the death of her husband.

 789 Bingo, *(Northern Arapaho Tribe of the Wind River Reservation).* One-hundred-fifteen miles southeast of Grand Teton National Park. (307) 856-3964.

APPENDIX

Casinos in Las Vegas

VISITORS INFORMATION:
Las Vegas Convention & Visitors Authority
3150 Paradise Road
Las Vegas, NV 89109
(702)687-4322

AIRPORT SLOTS
McCarran International Airport
5757 South Paradise Road
Las Vegas, NV 89119
(702)261-5743

ALADDIN HOTEL & CASINO
3667 Las Vegas Boulevard South
Las Vegas, NV 89109
(702)736-0111, (800)634-3424

ALGIERS HOTEL
2845 Las Vegas Boulevard South
Las Vegas, NV 89109
(800)732-3361

**ANTHONY'S CLUB CASINO,
QUALITY INN HOTEL**
377 East Flamingo Road
Las Vegas, NV 89109
(702)733-7777, (800)634-6617

ARIZONA CHARLIE'S HOTEL & CASINO
740 South Decatur Boulevard
Las Vegas, NV 89107
(702)258-5200, (800)342-2695

ART'S PLACE
532 East Sahara Avenue
Las Vegas, NV 89104
(702)737-1466

AZTEC INN & CASINO
2200 Las Vegas Boulevard South

Las Vegas, NV 89104
(702)385-4566

BALLY'S CASINO RESORT
3645 Las Vegas Boulevard South
Las Vegas, NV 89109
(702)739-4591, (800)634-3434

BARBARY COAST HOTEL & CASINO
3595 Las Vegas Boulevard South
Las Vegas, NV 89132
(702)737-7111, (800)634-6755

BARCELONA HOTEL & CASINO
5011 East Craig Road
Las Vegas, NV 89115
(702)644-6300

BEANO'S CASINO
7200 West Lake Mead Boulevard
Las Vegas, NV 89128
(702)255-9150

BIG DOG'S BAR & GRILL
1511 North Nellis Boulevard
Las Vegas, NV 89101
(702)459-1099

BIG DOG'S BAR & GRILL
3025 Sheridan Street, Second Floor
Las Vegas, NV 89102
(702)368-3715

BIG DOG'S CAFE & CASINO
6390 West Sahara Avenue
Las Vegas, NV 89102
(702)876-3647

THE BIG GAME CLUB
4747 Fair Center Park
Las Vegas, NV 89102
(702)870-0087

**BINION'S HORSESHOE CLUB
HOTEL & CASINO**
128 Fremont Street
Las Vegas, NV 89109
(702)382-1600, (800)622-6468

BOARDWALK HOTEL & CASINO
3750 Las Vegas Boulevard South
Las Vegas, NV 89109
(702)736-2192, casino; (702)735-1167, hotel
(800)635-4581

BONANZA LOUNGE
430 East Bonanza Road
Las Vegas, NV 89110
(702)452-7955

BOOMTOWN HOTEL & CASINO & R.V. PARK
3333 Blue Diamond Road
Las Vegas, NV 89139
(702)263-7777, (800)588-7711

BOULDER STATION HOTEL & CASINO
4111 South Boulder Highway
Las Vegas, NV 89121
(702)432-7777, (800)683-7777

BOURBON STREET HOTEL & CASINO
120 East Flamingo Road
Las Vegas, NV 89109
(702)737-7200, (800)634-6956

CAESAR'S PALACE
3570 Las Vegas Boulevard South
Las Vegas, NV 89109
(702)731-7110, (800)634-6661

CALIFORNIA HOTEL & CASINO
12 Ogden Avenue
Las Vegas, NV 89125
(702)385-1222, (800)634-6255

CAPTAIN'S QUARTERS
2610 Regetta Drive
Las Vegas, NV 89128
(702)256-6200

CASINO ROYALE & HOTEL
3411 Las Vegas Boulevard South
Las Vegas, NV 89122
(702)737-3500

CASTAWAYS CASINO
3132 South Highland Drive
Las Vegas, NV 89109
(702)648-1961

CHARLIE'S LAKESIDE BAR & GRILL
740 South Decatur Boulevard
Las Vegas, NV 89107
(702)258-5170

CIRCUS CIRCUS HOTEL CASINO
880 Las Vegas Boulevard South
Las Vegas, NV 89109-1120
(702)734-0410, (800)444-CIRCUS

COIN CASTLE CASINO
15 East Fremont Street
Las Vegas, NV 89101
(702)385-7474

COTTIN PICKIN' BAR
3111 South Valley View J-104
Las Vegas, NV 89102

CONTINENTAL HOTEL
4100 Paradise Road
Las Vegas, NV 89109
(702)737-5555, (800)634-6641

COUNTRY LAND USA
2755 Las Vegas Boulevard South
Las Vegas, NV 89109

DAN'S ROYAL FLUSH CASINO
3049 Las Vegas Boulevard South
Las Vegas, NV 89109
(702)735-7666

DANNY'S SLOT COUNTRY
4213 Boulder Highway
Las Vegas, NV 89121
(702)451-4974

DAYS INN
707 East Fremont Street
Las Vegas, NV 89101
(702)388-1400, (800)325-2525

**DEBBIE REYNOLDS HOTEL, CASINO &
HOLLYWOOD MOVIE MUSEUM**
305 Convention Center Drive
Las Vegas, NV 89109
(702)734-0711, (800)633-1777

DRAFT HOUSE BAR & GRILL
4543 North Rancho Drive
Las Vegas, NV 89109
(702)645-1404

EL CORTEZ HOTEL & CASINO
600 East Fremont Street
Las Vegas, NV 89125
(702)385-5200, (800)643-6703

ELLIS ISLAND CASINO
4178 Koval Lane
Las Vegas, NV 89109
(702)733-8901

ERNIE'S CASINO
1901 North Rancho Drive

Las Vegas, NV 89106
(702)646-3447

EUREKA CASINO
595 East Sahara Avenue
Las Vegas, NV 89114
(702)794-3464

EXCALIBUR HOTEL & CASINO
3850 Las Vegas Boulevard South
Las Vegas, NV 89109
(702)597-7700, (800)937-7777

FITZGERALDS CASINO HOTEL
301 East Fremont Street
Las Vegas, NV 89101
(702)388-2400, (800)274-5825

FLAMINGO HILTON LAS VEGAS
3555 Las Vegas Boulevard South
Las Vegas, NV 89109
(702)733-3111, (800)732-2111

FOOTHILLS EXPRESS
714 North Rainbow Boulevard
Las Vegas, NV 89108
(702)878-2281

FOOTHILLS RANCH
3377 North Rancho Drive
Las Vegas, NV 89130
(702)658-6360

49ER SALOON & CASINO
1556 North Eastern Avenue
Las Vegas, NV 89101
(702)649-2421

FOUR QUEENS HOTEL & CASINO
202 East Fremont Street
Las Vegas, NV 89031
(702)385-4011, (800)634-6045

FREMONT HOTEL & CASINO
200 East Fremont Street
Las Vegas, NV 89101
(702)385-4011, (800)385-6229

FRIENDLY FERGIE'S CASINO & SALOON
2430 Las Vegas Boulevard South
Las Vegas, NV 89104
(702)598-1985

FRONTIER HOTEL & GAMBLING HALL
3120 Las Vegas Boulevard South
Las Vegas, NV 89109
(702)794-8200, (800)421-7806

GLASS POOL INN
4613 Las Vegas Boulevard South
Las Vegas, NV 89109
(702)739-6636, (800)527-7118

GLORIA'S II
1966 North Rainbow Boulevard
Las Vegas, NV 89108
(702)647-0744

GOLD COAST HOTEL & CASINO
4000 West Flamingo Road
Las Vegas, NV 89103
(702)367-7111, (800)331-5334

GOLD SPIKE HOTEL & CASINO
400 East Ogden Avenue
Las Vegas, NV 89101
(702)384-8444, (800)634-6703

THE GOLDEN GATE CASINO
1 East Fremont Street
Las Vegas, NV 89101
(702)382-6300, (800)426-6703

THE GOLDEN NUGGET HOTEL CASINO
129 East Fremont Street
Las Vegas, NV 89101
(702)634-3403, (800)634-3454

HACIENDA RESORT HOTEL & CASINO
3950 Las Vegas Boulevard South
Las Vegas, NV 89193
(702)798-8289, (800)634-6713

HARD ROCK HOTEL & CASINO
4455 Paradise Road
Las Vegas, NV 89170-0387
(702)693-5000, (800)HRD-ROCK

HARRAH'S LAS VEGAS
3475 Las Vegas Boulevard South
Las Vegas, NV 89109
(702)369-5000, (800)634-6765

HOLIDAY INN
325 East Flamingo Road
Las Vegas, NV 89109
(702)732-9110, (800)732-7889

HOLIDAY INN LAS VEGAS, BOARDWALK CASINO
3750 Las Vegas Boulevard South
Las Vegas, NV 89109
(702)735-1167

HOLY COW! CASINO, CAFE & BREWERY
2423 Las Vegas Boulevard South
Las Vegas, NV 89104
(702)732-7697

HOLY COW! CASINO, CAFE & BREWERY
3025 Sheridan Street
Las Vegas, NV 89041
(702)732-2697

CONTINENTAL HOTEL & CASINO
4100 Paradise Road
Las Vegas, NV 89109
(702)737-5555, (800)634-6641

HOTEL SAN REMO
115 East Tropicana Avenue
Las Vegas, NV 89109
(702)739-9000, (800)522-REMO

HOWARD JOHNSON ON TROPICANA
3111 West Tropicana Avenue
Las Vegas, NV 89103
(702)798-1111, (800)654-2000

IMPERIAL PALACE HOTEL & CASINO
3535 Las Vegas Boulevard South
Las Vegas, NV 89109
(702)731-3311, (800)351-7400

J.J.'S SIERRA CLUB
4350 Las Vegas Boulevard North
Las Vegas, NV 89115
(702)643-1955

JACKIE GAUGHAN'S PLAZA
1 Main Street
Las Vegas, NV 89101
(702)386-2110

KING 8 HOTEL & GAMBLING HALL
3330 West Tropicana Avenue
Las Vegas, NV 89103
(702) 736-8988, (800)634-3488

KLONDIKE INN & CASINO
5191 Las Vegas Boulevard South
Las Vegas, NV 89119
(702)739-9351

LADY LUCK CASINO HOTEL
206 North Third Street
Las Vegas, NV 89101
(702)477-3000, (800)523-9852

LAS VEGAS CLUB HOTEL & CASINO
18 East Fremont Street
Las Vegas, NV 89102
(702)385-1664, (800)634-6532

LAS VEGAS HILTON HOTEL & CASINO
3000 Paradise Road
Las Vegas, NV 89109
(702)732-5111, (800)732-7117

LEROY'S HORSE & SPORTS PLACE
114 South First Street
Las Vegas, NV 89101
(702)382-1561

THE LIFT BAR
3045 South Valley View Boulevard
Las Vegas, NV 89102
(702)364-0306

LITTLE CEASAR'S
3665 Las Vegas Boulevard
Las Vegas, NV 89109
(702)734-2827

LONGHORN CASINO
5288 Boulder Highway
Las Vegas, NV 89101
(702)345-9170

LOOSE CABOOSE SALOON
15 North Nellis Boulevard #A-1
Las Vegas, NV 89110
(702)452-4500

LUXOR HOTEL & CASINO
3900 Las Vegas Boulevard South
Las Vegas, NV 89119-1000
(702)262-4000, (800)288-1000

MAD MATTY'S BAR & GRILLE
8100 West Sahara Avenue
Las Vegas, NV 89117
(702)254-9997

MAIN STREET BAR & GRILL
650 South Main Street
Las Vegas, NV 89101
(702)387-1896, (800)782-8966

MARDI GRAS INN, BEST WESTERN
3500 Paradise Road
Las Vegas, NV 89109
(702)731-2020, (800)634-6501

MAXIM HOTEL & CASINO
160 East Flamingo Road
Las Vegas, NV 89109
(702)731-4300, (800)634-6987

**MGM GRAND HOTEL,
CASINO & THEME PARK**
3799 Las Vegas Boulevard South
Las Vegas, NV 89109
(702)891-1111

THE MIRAGE
3400 Las Vegas Boulevard South
Las Vegas, NV 89119
(702)791-7111

MISS LUCY'S GAMBLING HALL & SALOON
129 North Third Street
Las Vegas, NV 89121
(702)305-3131

MONTE CARLO
3770 Las Vegas Boulevard South
Las Vegas, NV 89119
(702)730-7777

MOULIN ROUGE HOTEL
900 West Bonanza Road
Las Vegas, NV 89106
(702)648-5054

NEVADA PALACE HOTEL & CASINO
5255 Boulder Highway
Las Vegas, NV 89122
(702)458-8810, (800)634-3995

NEW YORK NEW YORK
3790 Las Vegas Boulevard South
Las Vegas, NV 89109
(702)740-6969

NITE TWAIN LOUNGE
495 East Twain Avenue
Las Vegas, NV 89109
(702)732-4151

NOB HILL CASINO
3411 Las Vegas Boulevard South
Las Vegas, NV 89109
(702)458-8810

ONE-EYED JACKS #4
3400 Boulder Highway
Las Vegas, NV 89121

OPERA HOUSE CASINO
3411 Las Vegas Boulevard North
Las Vegas, NV 89030
(702)399-3000

O'SHEA'S
3555 Las Vegas Boulevard South
Las Vegas, NV 89109
(702)792-0777

P.J. RUSSO'S
2300 South Maryland Parkway
Las Vegas, NV 89104
(702)735-5454

P.T.'S BAR & GRILL
4424 Spring Mountain Road
Las Vegas, NV 89102
(702)227-0245

P.T.'S PUB
347 North Nellis Boulevard
Las Vegas, NV 89110
(702)437-8607, (702)452-9555

P.T.'S PUB
8584 West Lake Mead Boulevard
Las Vegas, NV 89128
(702)228-0758

P.T.'S PUB
4604 West Sahara Avenue
Las Vegas, NV 89102
(702)258-0224

P.T.'S PUB
1631 North Ranchero Drive
Las Vegas, NV 89106
(702)646-6657

P.T.'S PUB
2875 South Nellis Boulevard
Las Vegas, NV 89121
(702)641-1750

P.T.'S PUB
4825 West Flamingo Road
Las Vegas, NV 89103
(702)367-1606

PALACE STATION HOTEL & CASINO
2411 West Sahara Avenue
Las Vegas, NV 89102
(702)367-2411, (800)634-3101

PADDLEWHEEL HOTEL & CASINO
305 Convention Center Drive
Las Vegas, NV 89109
(702)734-0711, (800)782-2600

PEPPERMILL COFFEE SHOP & LOUNGE
2985 Las Vegas Boulevard South
Las Vegas, NV 89109
(702)346-5232

PIONEER CLUB
25 East Fremont Street
Las Vegas, NV 89101
(702)386-5000

PORT TRACK
3190 West Sahara Avenue
Las Vegas, NV 89102
(702)873-3345

QUALITY INN SUNRISE SUITES
4575 Boulder Highway
Las Vegas, NV 89109
(702)733-7777

QUEEN OF HEARTS HOTEL & CASINO
19 East Lewis Avenue
Las Vegas, NV 89101
(702)382-8878, (800)835-6005

R-BAR
6000 West Charleston Boulevard
Las Vegas, NV 89102
(702)259-0120

RAINBOW VEGAS HOTEL
401 South Casino Center Boulevard
Las Vegas, NV 89102
(702)386-6166

RIO SUITE HOTEL & CASINO
3700 West Flamingo Road
Las Vegas, NV 89103
(702)252-7777, (800)888-1808

RIVIERA HOTEL & CASINO
2901 Las Vegas Boulevard South
Las Vegas, NV 89109
(702)734-5110, (800)634-3420

ROYAL HOTEL & CASINO
99 Convention Center Drive
Las Vegas, NV 89109
(702)735-6117, (800)634-6666

SAHARA RESORT HOTEL & CASINO
2535 Las Vegas Boulevard South
Las Vegas, NV 89109
(702)737-2111, (800)634-6666

SAHARA SALOON
3345 East Sahara Avenue
Las Vegas, NV 89104
(702)457-2020

SAM'S TOWN HOTEL & GAMBLING HALL
5111 Boulder Highway
Las Vegas, NV 89122
(702)456-7777, casino; (702)458-0711,
hotel;
(800)456-0711

SANDS HOTEL & CASINO
3555 Las Vegas Boulevard South
Las Vegas, NV 89109
(702)733-5000, (800)634-6901

SANTE FE HOTEL & CASINO
4949 North Rancho Drive
Las Vegas, NV 89130
(702)658-4900, (800)872-6823

SASSY SALLY'S
32 Fremont Street
Las Vegas, NV 89101
(702)382-5777

SHALIMAR
1401 Las Vegas Boulevard South
Las Vegas, NV 89104
(702)388-0301

SHERATON DESERT INN RESORT & CASINO
3145 Las Vegas Boulevard South
Las Vegas, NV 89101
(702)733-4488, (800)634-6906

SHOWBOAT HOTEL & CASINO
2800 East Fremont Street
Las Vegas, NV 89104
(702)385-9123, (800)826-2800

SIERRA GAMBLING HALL
4350 North Las Vegas Boulevard
Las Vegas, NV 89115
(702)643-1955

SILVER CITY CASINO
3001 Las Vegas Boulevard South
Las Vegas, NV 89109
(702)732-4152

SILVER DOLLAR SALOON
2501 East Charleston Boulevard
Las Vegas, NV 89104
(702)382-6921

SKINNY DUGAN'S PUB
4127 West Charleston Boulevard
Las Vegas, NV 89102
(702)877-0522

SLOTS-A-FUN CASINO
2880 Las Vegas Boulevard South
Las Vegas, NV 89109
(702)734-1212

SMOKE RANCH JUNCTION
2425 North Rainbow Boulevard
Las Vegas, NV 89108
(702)656-1888

SPORT OF KINGS
365 East Convention Center Drive
Las Vegas, NV 89109
(702)893-3500

STAGE DOOR CASINO
4000 South Audrie Street
Las Vegas, NV 89109
(702)733-0124, (702)733-9876

STARDUST RESORT & CASINO
3000 Las Vegas Boulevard South
Las Vegas, NV 89109
(702)732-6111, (800)634-6757

STRATOSPHERE HOTEL CASINO
2000 Las Vegas Boulevard South
Las Vegas, NV 89104
(702)380-7707

SUPER 8 MOTEL
5288 Boulder Highway
Las Vegas, NV 89122
(702)435-8888, (800)825-0880

SUPER 8 MOTEL
4250 Koval Lane
Las Vegas, NV 89109
(702)794-0888, (800)800-8000

TOWN HALL CASINO, DAYS INN
4155 Koval Lane
Las Vegas, NV 89109
(702)731-2111, (800)634-6541

TREASURE ISLAND HOTEL & CASINO
3300 Las Vegas Boulevard South
Las Vegas, NV 89109
(702)894-7711, (800)634-6283

THE TRIPLE PLAY
1875 South Decatur Boulevard
Las Vegas, NV 89102
(702)364-0808

TROPICANA RESORT & CASINO
3801 Las Vegas Boulevard South
Las Vegas, NV 89109
(702)739-2222, (800)468-9494

UKELELE LOUNGE
620 Las Vegas Boulevard North
Las Vegas, NV 89101
(702)382-7364

UNION PLAZA HOTEL & CASINO
One Main Street
Las Vegas, NV 89101
(702)386-2110, (800)634-6575

VACATION VILLAGE HOTEL & CASINO
6711 Las Vegas Boulevard South
Las Vegas, NV 89119
(702)897-1700, (800)658-5000

VEGAS WORLD HOTEL & CASINO
2000 Las Vegas Boulevard South
Las Vegas, NV 89104
(702)382-2000, (800)634-6277

WEST HILL LANES
4747 West Charleston Boulevard
Las Vegas, NV 89102
(702)878-9711

WESTERN HOTEL & CASINO
889 Fremont Street
Las Vegas, NV 89101-4239
(702)384-4629, (800)634-6703

WESTWARD HO MOTEL & CASINO
2900 Las Vegas Boulevard South
Las Vegas, NV 89109
(702)731-2900, (800)634-6803

THE WHISTLE STOP
2839 West Sahara Avenue
Las Vegas, NV 89102
(702)873-2086

Casinos in Atlantic City

VISITORS INFORMATION:
Atlantic City Convention & Visitors Bureau
2314 Pacific Avenue
Atlantic City, NJ 08401
(609)348-7100, (800)262-7395

**BALLY'S PARK PLACE CASINO
HOTEL & TOWER**
The Boardwalk & Park Place
Atlantic City, NJ 08401
(609)340-2000, (800)BALLYS-7

CAESARS'S ATLANTIC CITY
2100 Pacific Avenue
Atlantic City, NJ 08401
(609)348-4411, (800)443-0104

CLARIDGE HOTEL CASINO
Indiana Avenue & The Boardwalk
Atlantic City, NJ 08401
(609)340-3400, (800)257-8585

THE GRAND, A BALLY'S CASINO RESORT
Boston at Pacific Avenues
Atlantic City, NJ 08401
(609)347-7111, (800)247-8677

HARRAH'S CASINO HOTEL
777 Harrah's Boulevard
Atlantic City, NJ 08401
(609)441-5000, (800)2-HARRAH

MERV GRIFFIN'S RESORT CASINO HOTEL
The Boardwalk at North Carolina Avenue
Atlantic City, NJ 08401
(609)344-6000, (800)336-MERV

SANDS HOTEL CASINO & COUNTRY CLUB
Indiana Avenue & Brighton Park
Atlantic City, NJ 08401
(609)441-4000, (800)257-8580

**SHOWBOAT HOTEL CASINO & BOWLING
CENTER**
801 Boardwalk at States Avenue
Atlantic City, NJ 08401
(609)343-4000, (800)257-8580

**TROPWORLD CASINO & ENTERTAINMENT
RESORT**
Iowa Avenue & The Boardwalk
Atlantic City, NJ 08401
(609)340-4000, (800)257-6227

TRUMP PLAZA HOTEL & CASINO
Mississippi Avenue & The Boardwalk
Atlantic City, NJ 08401
(609)441-6000, (800)677-7787

TRUMP TAJ MAHAL RESORT & CASINO
1000 Boardwalk at Virginia Avenue
Atlantic City, NJ 08401
(609)449-1000, (800)825-8786

TRUMP'S CASTLE HOTEL & CASINO
Huron Avenue & Brigantine Boulevard
Atlantic City, NJ 08401
(609)441-2000, (800)441-5551

GLOSSARY

ACTION: The betting

BACCARAT: Also known as Nevada Baccarat, Punto Banco, or American Baccarat. A high stake game usually played with eight decks of cards, sometimes six, with the objective of drawing cards as close to the nine as possible. The higher total of two opposing sides, the "player/punto" and "bank/banco" wins. The cards are shuffled by the croupier, cut by a player or croupier (or both), and dealt one by one from a shoe called the box. Players may bet on the bank or the player. The house banks all bets. No player is ever responsible for putting up the bank or for any wagers other than his/her own. However, the players take turns dealing the cards and acting as banker.

BET: The dollar amount a player is willing to risk in order to play the game.

BIG SIX *(Wheel of Fortune, Money Wheel)*: Consists of a wheel and a betting layout. The circular vertical wheel is around five feet in diameter, divided into equally spaced sections separated by a nail-like projection. A fixed flexible strap mounted above the top edge clicks past the post until the wheel stops. The flexible marker resting between two posts indicates the winner. The Nevada wheels and Atlantic City wheels have fifty-four sections, but slightly different pay-offs on the flag and the joker. Betting layouts vary, but all the layouts show the payoff odds.

BINGO: Played in the casinos of Nevada, but not in Atlantic City. The object is to match the numbers one to seventy-five, to eighty, or ninety on the drawn ping-pong balls to the twenty-five numbered spaces on the game card with the central space labeled free. The standard winning pattern in bingo consists of a completed vertical, horizontal or diagonal row, all four corners, or a "coverall" (or a "Blackout") covering all the numbers on the card.

BINGO CARD: Made of either paper or cardboard. Players must use the card in order to play the game.

BINBO DOBBER: A device with a round, sponge-like top that is turned upside down and squeezed to mark the numbers on the Bingo card as the numbers are called.

BLACKJACK (TWENTY-ONE): The term blackjack refers to a two-card holding of "21," an ace with any face card or a ten. The object is to get nearer to the total of "21," without exceeding it, than the dealer. The rules vary slightly from casino to casino as does the number of decks used in its play. It is one of the few games where the house advantage can be reduced to one-percent by correct play and the player has a reasonably good chance of winning a session.

BLACKJACK: A face card or a ten with an ace.

BLACKOUT: A specialty game played during a regular session of Bingo.

BONES: Dice.

BURN CARD: When the dealer discards the top card or cards from the top of a newly shuffled deck in order to throw professional card counters off.

BUST: In blackjack, a player's card total exceeds 21.

CARD STAND: Holds the Bingo card, allowing the player to view the cards rapidly.

CARIBBEAN STUD POKER: A five-card poker game. To play, each player antes, with the option of betting an extra dollar for a progressive jackpot and receives five cards face down. The dealer gets five cards one of which is face up. The player then examines his hand and decides either to fold, forfeiting the ante, or to play thereby making an additional bet exactly doubling his ante. The dealer can only play with an Ace, King or better. If the dealer cannot open, the player automatically wins the ante, and that hand is over.

CHIP RACK: A rack in front of the dealer that separates the different denominations of chips. The chips are arranged in order from smallest to the largest denomination of chips used at that table.

CHUCK-A-LUCK: A game also known as Nevada Chuck-a-luck, Grand Hazard, or Hazard, played in Nevada casinos with three dice spun round in a hourglass-shaped contraption called a "chuck cage" and a betting layout. The casino edge is dependent upon the bet ranges from 2.8% to 30.6%. Long a staple of Nevada casinos, it has been generally replaced by the "Big Six" wheel.

CRAPS: A two dice game played at a table with high sides. Bets are made with chips placed on an appropriate area of the layout. There are different types of craps, but the American version of Bank Craps is the standard casino game. All player bets are banked by the casino. The house advantage, depending upon the wagers placed, ranges from 0.8% to 16.7%.

DEALER'S DOWN CARD: In blackjack, one of the two cards dealt by and to the dealer that is placed face down so that the players at the table cannot see its value.

DEALER'S UP CARD: In blackjack, one of the two cards dealt by and to the dealer that is placed face up so that all the players at the table can see its value.

DEUCE: A die with two spots.

DIAMONDS: A specialty game sometimes played during a regular session of Bingo.

DISCARD TRAY: The plastic tray to the right of the dealer that holds all the used cards. This tray keeps the cards out of the playing area on the table and prevents them from accidentally being used again.

DOUBLING DOWN: In blackjack, when a player is dealt two cards that equal ten or eleven, s/he may double the bet and the dealer will give the player one card. The more advanced player usually tries to keep a mental note of how many face cards have been dealt. The objective is to get a face card so that his/her card count will add up to twenty or twenty-one. Some casinos will allow a player to "Double Down" on any two cards. Other casinos will allow it to take place only when the player had a ten or an eleven.

DOWN CARD: In blackjack, the last card on the table to be turned up by the dealer.

EARLY BIRD SESSION: A certain number of games that are played prior to the start of a regularly scheduled session of Bingo.

FACE CARD: A king, queen or jack in a deck of cards; a ten-count card.

FIRST BASE: The first seat at a blackjack table, usually to the extreme left of the dealer.

HALF A YARD: Fifty U.S. dollars.

HAND: One deal in a card game; the cards held by player.

HIGH ROLLER: Bettor who plays with large amounts of money.

HIT: When players ask for more cards because they feel their hand is not strong enough in value to beat the dealer's. The only time the player cannot request additional cards is if the player has Doubled Down or Split aces.

HOUSE (THE HOUSE): The operators of the casino gambling games.

HOUSE RULES: The rules the casino requires each player and blackjack table to follow.

INSURANCE: The only time a player will be offered insurance in the game of blackjack is when the dealer's up card is an ace. At that time, the player may add an amount equal to half of the player's original bet. If the dealer has a blackjack, everyone at the table loses their original bets, unless a player happens to have a blackjack to tie the dealer. The players who have purchased insurance to cover their bets will be paid two to one for their insurance bets and will lose their original bets. If the dealer does not have blackjack, the insurance bets are lost to the house, and the table continues to play out the cards on the table.

JACKPOT: In slots, the top money payout on a machine.

JUNKET: An organized group trip to a casino for players who receive complimentaries, i.e., transportation, rooms, food, drinks, in exchange for a certain amount of playing time and a specific minimum wager.

JUNKET OPERATOR: Occasionally a casino employee or representative, but most often an independent operator who organizes the junket.

"LET IT RIDE" STUD POKER: A game based on five card stud poker. Players do not play against the dealer or any other player. Each player places three equal bets. Each player receives three cards, the dealer takes two cards at the conclusion of the deal. The object is to get a good poker hand using the three cards and the dealer's two cards. After looking at the first three cards, the player may ask for his/her first bet back or they may "Let It Ride." The dealer then burns the top card and exposes the first community card. The player may then ask for his/her second bet back or "Let It Ride." After the second bet, all players must tuck their cards under the third wager. The dealer then burns another card and exposes the second community card. The dealer exposes and then pays all winning hands according to the payout schedule. Players cannot discuss or show their hands to each other. If a player's hand has more or less than three cards, that hand is dead.

KENO: A mechanical game where the objective is to pick out a set of numbers one to eighty, twenty of which will be selected at random in each game. One number pays two–one odds of three–one,

which gives the casino a twenty-five-percent edge. The more numbers a player picks, the longer the odds. Players mark their choice of numbers on the Keno ticket and place their wagers at the Keno counter or with a keno girl. Eighty numbered ping-pong balls held in a transparent container known as the Keno "goose" are blown out randomly one at a time to produce the winning numbers. Consequently, the game requires no skill, just luck to select winning numbers.

LETTING IT RIDE: Leaving the original bet on the table along with the winnings on the previous hand and betting them again.

LIMIT: The maximum amount a person can wager.

MAIN BOARD: The monitor located directly above the caller and the Bingo machine. Monitors are located throughout the Bingo hall.

MARKER: An IOU in a casino.

MEGA BINGO: A new type of Bingo that connects Bingo halls electronically across a specific area.

MINI-BACCARAT: The form of baccarat with relatively low limits played on a miniature size table where only the house dealer deals the cards and banks all bets for the casino. All players may wager on either the bank, the player's hand, or a tie.

MULTIPLE ACTION BLACKJACK: Allows players to play up to three hands at a time and to make three wagers all from the same seat. The dealer plays the same top card for all three hands.

NATURAL : When the dealer deals an ace and a face card of the same suit to any player or players. There can be multiple naturals dealt to players at one table.

ONE-ARMED BANDIT: Slot machine.

PAI GOW POKER: Classic western poker blended with the oriental game Pai Gow. It is played with a regular fifty-two card deck plus one Joker. The Joker can be used only as an Ace, or to complete a Straight or Flush or a Straight Flush. Pai Gow Poker gives the player a chance to turn the tables on the house by giving each player the opportunity to "bank" the bets against all the other players, including the dealer.

The object of the game is to have both your hands score higher than both hands of the bank. Hands rank the same as regular poker hands. Upon receiving seven cards, the player must arrange them into two separate hands: a two-card "second highest" or "low" front hand and a five-card "highest" or "high" back hand. A player wins the bet if both hands are higher than the banker's hands. A player loses the bet if both hands are lower than the banker's hands. The player "pushes" if one hand wins and one hand loses. If either hand is exactly the same as the banker's hand, this is a tie and the banker wins all ties. All winning bets are charged a five-percent commission.

PAYOUT OR SLOT CHART: Listed on the front of the slot machine, telling what players will be paid if they play one coin and hit certain types of symbols.

PIT BOSS: A casino employee who supervises a gaming pit, which consists of eight to fifteen tables. The pit boss will make a final decision for the dealer if problems arise regarding the way the cards were dealt.

POINT: Any number or total gambling game that is wagered on.

POKER: A popular card game of several forms played in legal cardrooms and casinos in the U.S. and a number of foreign casinos. Draw poker is the simplest form of the game. The principle Nevada casino versions are "Seven-Card Stud" and "Texas Hold-em." The objective of poker is to win the pot by either exposing the best hand at the final showdown, or being the last player left in the hand which happens when a player forces the other players out by making a final bet that no other player calls.

PREMIUM PLAYER: Generally a high roller, depending upon the casino, who has cash or a credit line of around $2,500 to gamble.

PROGRESSIVE BINGO: A Bingo game that allows for a certain number of balls to be called each time the game is played. If no one has won after all the alloted numbers have been called, the jackpot will grow by increments as a certain amount of extra numbers are called.

PUSH OR TIE: In blackjack, when the dealer's card total and the player's card total are of equal value. Neither the dealer nor the player loses when this occurs.

RF&B: Room, Food and Beverage: Players who have "RF&B" are very big players who have qualified for this service many times.

ROULETTE: A game of pure chance in which luck is the dominate element. The double-zero American version of thirty-eight numbers includes zero (0) and double zero (00). There are eight different classes of bets with 161 alternatives and the loss of all even money bets when the zero or double zero appears.

SCARED MONEY: Hard-earned money; money that can't afford to be lost.

SDS SYSTEM: A slot tracking system in which the player inserts a plastic card into a "reader" in order to record how long s/he plays and how much money s/he deposits into the machine. The player will receive credit for playing her/his time.

SHOE: In blackjack, the device that holds cards.

SHOOTER: In craps, the person who throws the dice.

SIX PACK: A specialty game played sometimes during a regular session of Bingo.

SLOT CLUBS: Incentive programs offered by casinos to get players to come back to the casino. The majority of slot clubs are free and the member must insert his or her membership card into the slot machine. During the member's session at the machine, points are acquired, which can be redeemed for cash, prizes, free meals, free rooms and other gifts.

SLOTS: Mechanical and computerized game machines known as "one arm bandits" in the U.S. In the U.S. the twenty-five cent and $1 machines dominate, but nickel, dime, and half-dollar machines are also available. $5, $25, and even $100 machines have been introduced in the U.S. The more traditional machines consist of Fruit-Symbol and Jackpots-only machines. The computerized electronic video machines include video poker, blackjack, keno, roulette, dice, bingo, etc. Any number of machine units, mechanical or electronic, may be linked together to one progressive meter to offer progressive jackpots that increase with each play of a linked machine. In Super Jackpot machines, the major prize winning combination is a fixed amount that is substantially greater than it ordinarily would be if the single coin payoff were simply multiplied by the number of coins played. Players are induced to deposit the maximum number of coins to win a Super Jackpot. Super Jackpots are often over a million dollars.

SPLINTERS: Individual players brought in by the casino to gamble. Most often they arrive independently, but are sometimes hooked up with a junket.

SPLITTING PAIRS: In blackjack, a player may split two cards of identical value into two separate hands and wager each hand separately.

STACKING: When a player makes a bet, the dealer will stack the chips in a particular order according to their monetary value.

STAND: In blackjack, to refuse to take another card.

STICK, STICKMAN: In craps, the casino employee who pushes dice from player to player (with a long stick) calls out the numbers thrown, and controls the pace of the game.

SUCKER BET: An ill-advised wager.

SURRENDER: An option not offered by all casinos in the game of blackjack. Players have the right to surrender their cards and give up half of their original bet if they feel the dealer is going to win. Surrender can happen only on the first two cards dealt. The player waits until the next round of cards to place a bet.

TABLE RULES: The standard each player must follow while playing at a casino table.

TABLE CHART: The chart on which the caller places the ball after it is called to the players. Once the ball is placed on the chart, the monitors around the Bingo hall will light up that space to reflect that the ball has been called.

TAPPED: To be out of money.

THIRD BASE: Blackjack player who sits on the far right of the table. The last player to receive any cards.

WHALE: An ultra-high roller with a credit line in excess of $50,000.

WOOD: Gamblers without money.

MASTER INDEX

A

Abasaloka Casino 175
Absecon Island 15
Absentee Shawnee 137
Acomita, NM 210
Ada, OK 132
Adams Memorial Museum 141
Agency Village, SD 139
Agua Caliente Band of Cahuilla
    Indians 163
Ak-Chin Indian Community 154
Aladdin 187, 196, **197**
Alameda County Fairgrounds 164
Albany, CA 157
Albuquerque, NM 210
All American Futurity 212
Alpine, CA 157
Alton Belle Riverboat Casino 65, **66**
Alton, IL 65
Altoona, IA 105
American Indian Exposition 131
Ameristar Casino Vicksburg 57-58
Ameristar II 107
Anacortes, WA 218
Anadarko, OK 131
Annette Island 151
Apache Nation 131
Apache Nugget Casino 211
Apostle Islands National Lakeshore 95, 99
Aqueduct **24**, 25
Arabia Steamboat Museum 117
Arapaho Nation 132
Arapaho Park 166
Arcadia, CA 157
Argosy Casino (Kansas City, MO) 117
Argosy Casino (Lawrenceburg, IN) 76
Arikara 130
Arizona State Lottery 152
Arlington Heights, IL 66

Arlington Heights International
    Racecourse 66
Arthur, Chester A. 45
Assiniboine and Sioux Tribes of the Fort
    Peck Reservation 176
Atlantic City, NJ 15, 179
Atlantic City Race Course 22
Atlantis Casino Resort 207
Atmore, AL 33
Auberry Big Sandy Rancheria 158
Auberry, CA 158
Auburn, WA 218
Aurora, CO 166
Aurora, IL 66
Avi Hotel Casino 203

B

Baby Doe's Silver Dollar Casino 168
Bad River Band of Lake Superior
    Chippewa 99
Bad River Casino 99
Bad River Reservation 98
Bally's Belle of Orleans Casino 47
Bally's Las Vegas 192
Bally's Park Place 17
Bally's (Reno, NV) 206
Bally's Saloon and Gambling Hall 56
Balmoral Park 67
Baltimore, MD 11
Bangor May, ME 10
Bangor Raceway 10
Baraboo, WI 95
Baraga County Tourist and Recreation
    Association 79
Baraga, MI 78, 79
Baraga State Park 79
Barbary Coast 196
Barksdale Air Force Base 43

M

N

ESTABLISHMENT INDEX

The Establishment Index lists entries by type of establishment: bingo, casinos, harness and thoroughbred racing tracks, jai alai, lottery, museums, Native American gaming, parks, and river boats.

Harness Racing

Jai Alai

Lottery

Museums

Native American Gaming

Triple Crown